THE BUDAPEST BALLET

GÉZA KÖRTVÉLYES—GYÖRGY LŐRINC

THE BUDAPEST BALLET

THE BALLET ENSEMBLE OF THE HUNGARIAN
STATE OPERA HOUSE

CORVINA PRESS

EDITED BY GYÖRGY LŐRINC

ARTISTIC ADVISER: ZSUZSA KUN

APPENDIX COMPILED BY G. P. DIENES

TRANSLATED BY G. P. DIENES AND ÉVA RÁCZ

TRANSLATION REVISED BY ELISABETH WEST

FOREWORD

It was only after a long struggle for recognition that the art of ballet came into its own in Hungary. For many years it had been quite overshadowed by that older art to which it is so closely related, opera. But indeed, this can be said of ballet in most Central European countries in the nineteenth century and even as late as the middle of the twentieth century.

It was during the nineteen-thirties that Hungarian ballet began to develop under the powerful stimulus of a twofold discovery: the Hungarian folk dance and the Russian ballet. An awakened interest in the Hungarian folk dance followed naturally and inevitably the research into folk music and folk dance undertaken by Béla Bartók and Zoltán Kodály. And while the exploration and application of folk art gave an internal impulse to the development of the art of dancing, the Russian ballet was the decisive external influence to give it momentum. László Márkus, former director of the Budapest Opera House, writing in the late 1930s, commented on Hungarian ballet as follows: "All ancient arts are integrated, pure, logical and realistic in texture. Such is folk dancing, and such is the style of Russian ballet. And this is the style Hungarian ballet is seeking, a new art for us, which came into being under the guidance of the Russians."

The director of the Opera not only recognized this aim, he actively helped to realize it. He appointed two gifted artists to take charge of the ballet company at the Opera House: the choreographer, Gyula Harangozó, in 1936, and the ballet master, Ferenc Nádasi, in 1937. Together they fostered the development, at the Opera House, of the company which is the subject of this book. It was they who revived the Budapest Ballet.

Both opera and ballet found a home, albeit independently, at the present Opera House which had been founded in 1884. There the art of ballet was first introduced by a number of foreign masters, most of them Italian. Campilli, Smeraldi, and Mazzantini were followed by Guerra in the dual role of choreographer and ballet master. He it was who taught, among other young Hungarians, Emília Nirschy, Anna Pallay and Ferenc Nádasi. After Guerra's departure in 1914, the ballet company at the Hungarian Opera House declined for many years.

Ferenc Nádasi was the first "master" of the present company. When he set to work, personal assets such as charm, gracefulness, good looks, the ability to smile alluringly or pantomime extravagantly, were all relegated to their proper place as of secondary importance; professional skill came to be regarded as of the highest value. The exacting internal laws that govern the art of ballet, and a strictly truthful attitude to the material of ballet, came to prevail over an earlier idiom of movement which had been divested of its original content. The playfulness associated with amateur or provincial dancing was eliminated and a professional standard established. Ferenc Nádasi proved to be a "master" in the old, classical sense of the term: a great teacher of art, capable of founding a school and establishing a company. Nádasi, in his role as teacher, trained the artists so that they were capable of interpreting and rendering the works in contemporary idiom. These contemporary works were then handed over to the dancers —one might almost say "cast at their feet"—by Gyula Harangozó. The works which thus came into being were based on Fokine's ideas for a ballet revival, the principles of which were incorporated in works performed all over the world by the famous Diaghilev company. Gyula Harangozó did not imitate, he merely adopted—or re-invented—the principles, for it is a well-known fact that progressive artists have a way of discovering what is timely even when they are working independently one of another.

Gyula Harangozó was already working within the framework of Fokine's creative principles when he formulated his very first work inspired by folk dance; he gave to this work the steps, the depth of feeling and the joy in dancing that is found in folk dancing. He was a creative artist and it was with the energy of the true artist that he devised one after another, in rapid succession, a series of ballets; from a group of dancers he created an ensemble, and helped them to establish rules and customs of their own. It is given only to the truly creative director to gather around himself the kind of integrated group of artists which from then on gradually developed into the ballet company of the Hungarian State Opera House. He was truly creative, a man trusted by the artists, for he knew what he wanted, was able to realize what he wanted, and what he realized was crowned with success.

From 1950 onwards the Budapest Ballet was continually enriched by the achievements of the Soviet ballet. Soviet choreographers brought to the stage in Budapest the finest creations of Soviet ballet, in both the classical and romantic traditions. And the foremost ballet masters of Moscow and Leningrad taught Hungarian artists the secrets of the "great style" essential for the rendering of these works.

Thus it became possible for the company to include a wide variety of ballets in their repertoire. As well as the ballets incorporating a national tradition, they were able to offer a classical repertoire; and so that all these works could be worthily interpreted, a well-trained and talented company was brought into being.

The way ahead is naturally our present concern. There are many alternative paths and it would be easy to miss the most promising. This is especially true at the present time when art is attracted to extremes and its definition is stretched to encompass activities which come close to a kind of dehumanization that is a denial of what we used to call art. The heritage of the past is re-assessed in every age, but today even this process is haphazard and chaotic. The art of dancing is especially vulnerable, for its master-pieces are not definitively recorded and there is therefore no authoritative tradition to protect it from rash and ill-advised attacks.

The Budapest Ballet is ranked among the great national companies, and its task is to address its art to as large an audience as possible made up of individuals from every section of society. Thus it is present-day taste that influences decisions about future developments in the company. Box-office success and favourable reception by the critics are two factors which enable the directors to assess what is popular: their conclusion is that there is a demand for two utterly different types of programme. The broad mass of the people would like one kind of programme; but there is also a demand for dancing that will satisfy a limited number of aesthetes, critics and theatre-goers.

The greater part of the audience seeks the emotional stimulus associated with theatre-going: they want to be stirred or amused, and they expect at the very least to be uplifted and given pleasure by the dancing. In ballet it is the quality of the dancing which is of prime importance. The costumes may be

6

splendid, the music excellent, the libretto outstanding, but all to no purpose if the dances are not good enough, if the dancing and production fail to give pleasure. But if the dances are genuinely good and expressive of man and his world, the work gives a sense of adventure even if other aspects of the production are below standard.

The needs of the minority are not so simple. They demand not "truth and humanity" but novelty and innovation. They are prepared to accept modifications by which dancing loses its very essence as an individual art, and all for the sake of introducing a so-called "radically" new element. Dance alienated from dance is the "ideal", and it is the anti-dance elements which arouse enthusiasm.

The Budapest Ballet is committed to the demands of the majority and is therefore under an obligation to develop along the same general lines as hitherto, while at the same time aiming at an ever higher standard of attainment. Below we give an account of the manner in which the company seeks to achieve its aim.

The Hungarian folk dance continues to exert an influence on the Budapest Ballet today but only indirectly. Folk costume is not customary nor does the décor exploit the romantic tradition of peasant settings; and the choreographies do not adopt the steps and motifs of the folk dances unaltered. But both the performing artists and the audiences prefer works that are full of feeling and closely related to real life rather than works full of abstractions. The performing artists cannot be really and truly "modern" in the expression of indifference. Their every gesture and movement is lyrical or dramatic like those of Hungarian peasants when they dance. Thus the lyricism and drama of the Budapest Ballet remains closely and deeply related to the Hungarian folk dance.

Likewise Soviet ballet, or if you wish, the foremost tradition of international ballet, continues to influence the art of the Budapest Ballet today. The company cherishes the classical works of choreographic literature, keeps them in its repertoire and their classical productions rank high even by international standards. These traditional works set the standard and are a continual source of instruction to the dancers, helping them to acquire the background knowledge and professional skill needed for the performance of new works.

Between 1962 and 1966 the Budapest Ballet presented a number of experimental works. The artists were given "a free hand", and the audience sat in judgment. Some of the good contemporary works were kept in the programme and found a place in the repertoire if they appealed to the audience. Both the negative and the positive results of these experiments served to guide the management in their policy for the future. A national ballet company is a museum in the best sense of the term: it displays and preserves the international and national treasures of the art of dancing. But it is at the same time an exhibition hall where the latest works, even experimental works, can be seen.

All this clearly shapes the character of the company; and its aims have been determined as follows:
– to enrich the repertoire with traditional masterpieces;
– to foster the national tradition, reviving Hungarian works and keeping them in the repertoire;
– to continue the introduction of the best foreign works to the Hungarian stage;
– to present in addition many kinds of new works, so that the younger generation of Hungarian choreographers can show their talents, and to encourage above all the production at a high standard, of works which employ contemporary techniques to carry on the national tradition.

Autumn, 1968   *György Lőrinc*

Editorial work on the text and illustrations was completed at the end of 1968. First nights, revivals, guest performances and changes in the staff that have taken place since are included in the Appendix and footnotes.

The publisher

THE REPERTOIRE OF THE BUDAPEST BALLET

The history of the ballet provides evidence that its development is most marked during periods of dynamic change and upheaval. The twentieth century has had its share of strain and conflict, both social and political, with the greater part of the world in a state of unrest, and in this tense atmosphere of dissatisfaction the art of expressive movement has developed as never before.

In every sphere of ballet—music, choreography, dancing skill and technique—there has been progress. There have been developments in all the various styles of ballet, and the art of dancing has by now cast its magic spell over the greater part of the five continents. Ballet has come into its own as an art which most truly expresses the age in which we live. Ballet has become truly international, but at the same time many new national ballet companies have emerged for the first time and there has been a great revival of interest in both national and folk dances.

During the last fifty years we have seen the emergence of a modern idiom, traditions have been challenged, there have been ambitious projects on a national and international scale, dances have been given philosophical and abstract meaning, and in spite of the fact that new trends have struggled into existence, orthodox classical dancing has held its own. The history of the art of ballet in our own times has been eventful and varied, as eventful and varied as the history it reflects.

This was the period that brought into being a modern national ballet in Hungary. We have so far seen two distinct eras in the history of Hungarian ballet, that of the period before the birth of the new Hungary, and that which has developed since that date. It would be interesting to trace the history of dancing during the last forty years in this country, but that would be to stray from the subject of this book which is the Budapest Ballet as we find it today, at the Hungarian State Opera House, a company which is the chief exponent of the art of ballet in Hungary.

It is an unrewarding task to write about dancing, for this ephemeral art lives only in the moment during which it casts its spell; it eludes verbal formulation and makes no concessions to the writer's wish to describe what he sees. It is left to the camera to come to his aid, for it is possible to photograph characteristic moments of the continuous poetic movement that constitutes a ballet. A successful combination of descriptions and photographs can offer something of the flavour of a stage performance, but even this scarcely approximates to the reality. Therefore the authors hope for nothing more than to stimulate the reader's interest in Hungarian ballet or, in the case of those who have already seen some of the repertoire, to help them to recapture the experience in memory.

Yet there are aspects of the art of ballet that are particularly well conveyed through the medium of description and photography: if not the living dance itself yet the part played in its creation by the individual artists, the technique of the dance, its theme and message, its characteristic patterns and stylistic features—which come to life only when the dancers practise and perform together to the sound of the music, in their costumes, on stage and behind the footlights.

And so we must now comment on that constantly changing selection of works, the repertoire, for this is what gives character to any great national company; this is what reveals a very important aspect of their art. We should not forget that this complex art combines within itself music, choreography, stage design and dancing; we must remember that it is possible to emphasize only one of these elements. Nevertheless we must make an attempt to introduce the repertoire of the Budapest Ballet.

Let us then start on a sightseeing tour—just as we would make the rounds of any museum or gallery—of the repertoire of the Hungarian Ballet, tracing the trends, and following its logical development, artistically and aesthetically, under the direction of successive choreographers, Hungarian or foreign. The following summary is not strictly chronological: a chronology will be found in the Appendix.

A true account of the Budapest Ballet must show the way in which the artists have become closely associated with particular works, a logical process which has helped to shape the range of choreography and variety of styles found in Hungarian ballet; certainly this provides a peculiarly national interpretation of the artistic trends of the century.

By virtue of their artistic merit, strength of conviction and sheer numerical superiority, the choreographies of Gyula Harangozó dominate the repertoire of the Budapest Ballet. Harangozó's works span the history of modern Hungarian ballet, for his dance creations, at once individual and yet emblematic of the national art of dance, have appeared over a period of several decades.

Harangozó is a choreographer with an original talent and he is also a gifted dancer of character parts. These two aspects of his art are inseparable, the one permeating and shaping the other and exerting simultaneously a similar influence on the character of the company. The development of his own dedicated career has been closely connected with the development of ballet in Hungary and throughout the world; it has been closely linked with the general trend of development in the arts in Hungary. When Harangozó began to apply his creative talents to the art of choreography, Harangozó the dancer was already one of the most outstanding artists in the company. It was at about this time, in the 1930s, that the achievement of the Russian Ballet—which had only just been dissolved—was gaining universal recognition. At the same time, a national ballet was coming into existence in a number of countries, while in other countries an established national art was being revived, dancers were being trained to perform their own national works and these were once again being performed in public.

This process was also initiated at the State Opera House in Budapest where the kind of development described above has continued right up to the present time. Those who initiated and pioneered this development, a difficult task of historic significance, were Harangozó and Ferenc Nádasi, the great Hungarian ballet master. New, up-to-date ballets that were essentially Hungarian in character were brought to life by a company that could boast of not a few outstanding solo dancers, and all this was accomplished at a time when Béla Bartók and Zoltán Kodály, internationally recognized as classical composers in the sphere of contemporary Hungarian music, were still doing creative work, an inspiration to everyone connected with art of any kind in Hungary.

The way ahead for the Budapest Ballet was also made clear by a fusing of Russian ballet with the more primitive, vigorous and essentially Hungarian folk art; this fusion defined the ideal for which they were struggling. In his own work Gyula Harangozó was inspired by both traditions. He has given us his own account of his development as follows:

"Particular trends in the art of ballet reached us only after considerable delay. The revolutionary innovations which gave new life to the ballet in Europe date from the year 1909. But in our own country *Princess Althea* and *Prince Argyle* were still being produced in 1921 and 1924 respectively. (These were popular ballets based on folk art and representing the old order in approach, music and dance.)

"The choreography of the first modern Russian ballet, Manuel de Falla's *The Three-cornered Hat*, did not reach Hungary until 1928. By that time, I had already spent two years at the Opera House, occasionally acting as an extra; and when the *Nutcracker* had its première in 1927, I danced the part of Trepak. But I was still a young student and I danced merely for the fun of it and because I enjoyed it. I had no intention of making a career as a dancer, having been quite unimpressed by any of the ballets I had so far seen. I thought very little of the mannered naiveté of the performances with their endless pantomime and *pas de deux*. The première of *The Three-cornered Hat* made me completely change my opinion. I was surprised—and very happy—to see that in the art of ballet there could exist a logical dramaturgy, characters with a reality of their own, pantomime that could be truly described as dancing, and so on. This work made me enthusiastic about the art of dancing and committed me, albeit unconsciously, to the trends initiated by Fokine, Massine and Balanchine. It was with the production of *The Three-cornered Hat* that Hungarian ballet was launched into an era of progress in which it quickly made up for a slow start." ("The Development of Hungarian Ballet" in *Táncművészet*, September 1956.)

The trends mentioned here were developed by Harangozó continuously throughout his lifetime and are discernible in all his productions. The individual works were created at long intervals of time sometimes lasting for years, but they are all related to each other; the specific character of each work was determined by a particular artistic aim, for he worked in a variety of different styles and genres. Only the best have survived the judgment of time and we intend to consider here only the most characteristic of Harangozó's works which are still in the repertoire of the company.

There may well be something symbolic about the fact that Harangozó's first ballet was a one-act ballet based on a Hungarian folk tale, *Scene in the Csárda* (music by Jenő Hubay); some fifteen years later the master used the same theme for his first full-length ballet, *Kerchief* (music by Jenő Kenessey). Both versions were for many years included in the programmes at the Opera, and this was not the result of haphazard selection but rather to meet popular demand, for audiences were completely won over by these first splendid adaptations of a popular Magyar tale, with Magyar music and Magyar dances. Today the company frequently includes an excerpt from the second of these ballets in its programmes of selected works, usually the great love duet between the gipsy couple against the background of a Hungarian village at olden times with a number of admirably defined characters—the Innkeeper's Wife, the Bailiff, the Hungarian Sweethearts, the Gipsy Couple, the harvesters and the policemen. These dances skilfully combine the national idiom with the classical tradition.

In *Kerchief* Harangozó used his choreographical gifts to incorporate in the ballet elements of a traditional Hungarian peasant dance and to some degree its spirit too—a thematic and stylistic task which challenged the creative imagination of the choreographer more than once. Of his later efforts in this direction we should mention another ballet inspired by folk dance, a pleasantly fluent and gay work called *Mischievous Students* (music by Ferenc Farkas), which is today the most important of Harangozó's creations in this style. The setting of this comedy is the historic Hungarian city of Debrecen during the nineteenth century. We are shown a variety of characters—in the manner of the short story by Mór

Jókai, the popular Hungarian romantic writer—the students at the College of Debrecen as they become involved in a number of colourful and adventurous episodes. Harangozó is very much at home in this setting: he devises a succession of scenes, full of interest and humour and the dancing is truly Hungarian in flavour and is complemented by excellent pantomime. Dance and mime are successfully blended, and the ballet gives sustained delight on account of its high spirits and infectious cheerfulness. The majority of the dances—except for the more stylized love duet—catch the spirit and rich forms of the Hungarian folk dance even more successfully than do the dances in Harangozó's earlier works. We see the herdsmen erupt from the crowds at the fair to dance their own wild dance in which the flicking and brandishing of the long ornamental whips plays an important part; there is the attempt to recruit some of the begowned students with their long-stemmed pipes and the tipsy solo of the eager-beaver of a student, the villain of the piece who tries to obstruct the path of true love. These characters are seen in the students' own den, an attractive setting made vivid in a series of splendid dances featuring much by play. Harangozó's dances that are folk art in character are the most successful, both stylistically and dramatically; and this was not due to chance inspiration, but much more to the fact that in 1949, when the ballet was composed, the Hungarian folk dance reached new heights of popularity. Everywhere in Hungary folk dancing in all its richness was to be seen on the stage and this experience of the unique art of folk dance added to the master's knowledge and made him even more attached to it as a creative art.

The creative approach evident in *Mattie the Gooseboy* (music by Ferenc Szabó), a full-length ballet first produced in 1960, reveals the same artistic principle as that on which the earlier pieces were based. The ballet depicts the adventures of Mattie the Gooseboy, a popular folk hero, the Hungarian people's Till Eulenspiegel, as he seeks for justice and revenge. Here the choreographer makes use of the more novel aspects seen in stage productions of Hungarian folk dances, but the work lacks artistic conviction and except for a few scenes and dances the ballet is on the whole less successful than its predecessors. It was not only a single characteristic principle based on folk art that linked Harangozó's early and late works; they are also linked through the music and the fact that they all include typical Harangozó parts which have an important function in the work as a whole. In their intonation these works are connected with the world of music principally associated with the name of Zoltán Kodály. Individual though the pieces are, the music is linked to the recruiting tunes and peasant themes heard in Hungarian folk music, though each in its own way also draws on certain innovations found in twentieth-century compositions.

These works provide a splendid range of individual roles, their only similarity being that they are capable of being played by Harangozó himself—Eager-Beaver Joe in *Mischievous Students*, the cunning Bailiff in *Kerchief* and Squire Döbrögi, the haughty landlord in *Mattie the Gooseboy*: they are all typical stage personalities excellently characterized by Harangozó the choreographer, and equally well rendered by Harangozó the dancer. All these figures are amusingly grotesque, caricatured so that they are in dramatic contrast to the worthy heroes; they are carefully observed portraits in which gesture and stance are equally characteristic; they are given self-revealing dance motifs and each one of them demands from the dancer exceptional agility and critical understanding. This is a world at one and the same time life-like and fairy-tale-like, playful and gay, an enclosed and intimate world that comes nearer to farce and comedy than to high drama or tragedy, a world with a message which is easy to understand, transparently clear and simple. And the character of the hero is always well suited to the dramatic and choreographic style of the ballet. This is no happy accident: it is simply that the characters and the work itself are alike the imaginative creations of Gyula Harangozó, dancer and choreographer.

Truth to life and vivid characterization in the folk-tale tradition is, however, only one aspect of Harangozó's creative art, an aspect that is peculiarly Hungarian. There is another level of his work in which the intention and message are not so direct, where the themes and ideas are more stylized and philosophical. We are thinking of the symbolism in the two Bartók ballets, the fairy tale and the horrific pantomime, in both of which Bartók's genius brilliantly conveyed the very essence of certain ethical and human ideals, so that these ballets now rank among the noblest examples of the art of ballet.

The Wooden Prince is a fable with overtones of the folk tale, interwoven with symbolic elements and introducing the Nature Fairy. Bartók's intention was to resolve on the plane of poetry and in the spheres of the dream the problem of the relationship between a man and a woman—their meetings and the development of this relationship. The wooden puppet, an animated mockery of the poet-prince, imposes itself between the vain princess and the sincere prince, but it is exposed as the lifeless thing that it is, the obstacles imposed by Nature are overcome, and the lovers can at last become united.

But before lovers can be united they must travel a road so long that it can only be measured by death and negotiated by destruction—this is the philosophical idea at the heart of the other Bartók ballet, *The Miraculous Mandarin*. The message in this work is that the seemingly impossible can be achieved by the power of the human will, for the symbolic figure of the Mandarin triumphantly dominates the work. In the low den of the apaches he struggles for the fulfilment of his passion; and he successfully resists every attempt to destroy him until his love and death have ennobled and uprooted from her sinful haunts the Streetwalker who has been depraved and made unworthy of her fellow humans by the temptations of the great city.

It is a very complex theme, with several layers of meaning, and the greatness and depth of Bartók's music is a tremendous challenge to any choreographer. Gyula Harangozó grappled with the problems of *The Wooden Prince* several times, on each occasion improving and polishing his original choreography dating from 1939. His last version dates from 1958. Although even this cannot be regarded as definitive, over-all and in some of the more important details it does correspond closely to the music, and the ballet as a whole has a great deal to recommend it. And here too it is no accident that the climax of the choreography is reached through the wooden figure of the title, its puppet-like movements built up of folk-dance elements which admirably express the essence of the plot and music and satisfy all the requirements, direct and indirect, of this major role. The reader can guess that this is yet another addition to the already populous family of characters danced by Harangozó. This grotesque, mechanical yet individualized puppet, which fits so well into the general pattern of the folk dance, enriches with new features Harangozó's gallery of characters to whom it is nevertheless very happily related. In his designs for the hero, however, and those representing elements of Nature such as the trees of the forest or water, Harangozó was influenced by motifs found in classical, character and acrobatic dancing. It is a very different world, a very different atmosphere and very different ideas that are presented in *The Miraculous Mandarin*. This is the ruthless, anxiety-ridden world of today, in which there is tension and conflict between bitterly opposed factions. From the very beginning, in the pantomime of the apaches as they wait for a suitable victim, there is an atmosphere of impending violence. Their movements

13

are exaggerated, discordant and sometimes abruptly arrested. Their gestures are significant in that they create an atmosphere, but they scarcely convey meaning at all and later become almost naturalistic, straightforward pantomime. The movements of the Streetwalker are more conventional and dance-like than those of the other characters while the Mandarin himself is brought to life by means of powerful, exaggerated movements in every direction. Everything about him is larger than life—his strength, his self-control, his mounting desire—and finally his struggle for fulfilment. This is expressed by attitudes of silent, almost statuesque immobility and equally by the irresistible momentum of his silent pursuit of the girl. He cannot relax or resume strictly human proportions until he is united in harmony with the woman he has so long desired.

The Student and the Old Gallant, the principal figures in the two intermediary episodes, are not such extreme characters and their dancing is therefore more restrained. Here again our attention is held by a role that seems to have been brilliantly devised for Harangozó personally: that of the Old Gallant, an ageing Lothario, already stiff in the joints, but still set on a philandering adventure; a lewd but moneyless Lothario who attempts to gain the Streetwalker's favours by means of a trick. This is again a grotesque role with a grotesque blend of dancing and pantomime, a unique and grotesque version of a familiar role, individualized by the master.

This work, like *The Wooden Prince*, lay for a long time neglected in the choreographer's studio before it was at last permitted to reach the stage in its present form. The choreography was in fact finished in 1941, but the première was banned by the authorities in spite of the fact that the authors—Bartók included—agreed to alter the setting and transfer the action to the fabulous Orient. The sets finally accepted were in the nature of a compromise, yet the ballet was not allowed to reach the stage until 1945, after the liberation of Hungary; and thus *The Miraculous Mandarin* was at last shown to the world in this form, partly symbolic, at times almost naturalistic, but certainly a form which fulfils Harangozó's intentions when he first created it. Since that time the ballet has never been off the repertoire and is more frequently performed than any other modern one-act piece. This ballet has by now won the admiration of critics and audiences alike all over Europe.

The characteristic Harangozó style of choreography, with its own individual brand of modernity and bold realism, has had a lasting influence on a much wider range of works than those with a strictly national flavour. Inspired by Fokine and Massine, the first masters of the Russian Ballet, Harangozó composed original choreographies for several highly successful pieces which have been performed by the international ballet companies of the twentieth century, and this aspect of his work has also occupied him for several decades. His versions of the *Polovtsian Dances*, *Promenade Concert*, and *Sheherazade* are all notable works including new features which further enrich the wide range of his creative achievement. In the sweeping movements and almost primitive force of the character dances for which he created such a remarkable variety of striking designs in the *Polovtsian Dances* (music by Borodin), the earliest of the three works, there is ample evidence that a choreographer of significant talent is able to compose a series of dances conveying the atmosphere of folk art without reference to the original folk dances; his designs come out of his own wide knowledge of style. Harangozó was able to supply what was needed at that particular time—new colours and a richer variety of women's dances than were to be found in the original version written at a time when there was still a preponderance of women dancers in the Budapest Ballet.

14

Promenade Concert, one of the prototypes of the Harangozó style, is akin to the contemporary and widely-performed *Blue Danube* and other ballets in the style of Strauss. The setting is the Prater in Vienna, the story is light, gay and swift-moving, an animated tableau of the characteristic figures of the "happy pre-war days" as seen through the kindly mists of memory. There is of course the young poet and his blond sweetheart, the arrogant primadonna and the rich but jealous suitor, the shoemaker's apprentice and the policeman with the huge moustaches, as well as a host of waiters and governesses; and every one of this motley company moves in the magical and poetic atmosphere created by Johann Strauss's lilting and whirling waltzes. The characters are excellently observed and the dances quicken the pulse. Neither by temperament, inclination, nor compulsion as an artist was Harangozó drawn towards tragic librettos. Apart from *The Miraculous Mandarin*, *Sheherazade* (music by Rimsky-Korsakov) is the only one of his works with a tragic plot that is still performed. It was staged in 1959 and presents to us the exotic world of the Arabian Nights. The beautiful heroine is a prisoner in the Sultan's harem, and the hero a Moorish youth who is in love with her. The ballet includes ardent love scenes and a tremendous duet that is both passionate and technically exacting. There are also tense and dramatic individual scenes, in the manner of the Soviet ballet-dramas, which call for a very high standard of dancing and dramatic skill on the part of the performers. For all these reasons the ballet is assured of lasting success.

These Harangozó ballets served to introduce and establish in the repertoire of the Budapest Ballet the choreographic traditions which had taken root during the first twenty-five years of the century. They are splendid examples of works in which tradition is happily combined with modernity, in which a twentieth-century conception of choreography is combined with nineteenth-century music.

On the other hand, the romanticism of the classical-academic convention was quite alien to Harangozó's outlook. To that type of work he never turned for inspiration nor was it his custom to try to re-interpret or re-formulate such works. The only exception he made was the late romantic *Coppélia*, and his adaptation of this work is a magnificent artistic achievement.

Straightforward, simple situations are those which appeal most to Harangozó; he feels at home on the sunny side of the street, in those aspects of human existence which can be readily understood by any sincere and thoughtful person. It would seem that he does not care for mysticism and obscurity, tragedy and decadence; he is not interested in speculation or the abstract. No wonder then that he gave to the original *Coppélia* libretto a different meaning and character, and in so doing produced a highly original and attractive work. Once again Harangozó the dancer was largely responsible for this success for he personally danced the part of Coppélius in an original and delightfully humorous interpretation of that character. The hero of the title, a unique creation, casts a glow over the entire work and gives it a very special and subtle atmosphere.

Harangozó's Coppélius is not an evil and frightening eccentric who has set his face against all men and who has a god-like power to create new beings. This Coppélius does not so much inspire fear as laughter and his exalted ideas make him at times quite pathetic. He is like an explorer who has lost his bearings, for he has escaped from the world of man only to find himself bound by his own machines and inventions. He guards his treasures and secrets jealously and the only reason why he rages against the inquisitive young people is because they have "violated his shrine" and enticed away his cherished automat, the dancing girl; otherwise he wants only to be left to work in peace.

In this version the ballet is inevitably dominated by the figure of Coppélius, and reaches its climax in the second act. It is here, in Coppélius's "magic den", that Harangozó's highly original talent is given full play; here we see an ingenious and brilliant combination of dance and pantomime that is both expressive and harmonious, every movement intelligently, characteristically and carefully motivated.

There is, for instance, the splendid "orchestra", the proud achievement of the old Jack-of-all-trades whose "music" first astonishes and then amuses the young girls who have stolen into his house. And how movingly the ballet shifts to the mood of tragicomedy when these music-playing figures have been attacked by Francis in his fury, and lie ravaged and supine, jerkily continuing the spasmodic puppet dance, to the dismay and horror of poor Coppélius.

It is impossible to enumerate every one of the master's excellent notions or to describe all his admirably expressive character dances, but we must mention one short but brilliant Harangozó monologue which features all the most remarkable aspects of the dance-play. It is the scene in which Coppélius angrily bursts into the party which lends an air of festivity to the third act, and in one of his typical and expressive pantomimes "tells" all that happened in the previous act between the quarrelsome young people, Coppélia and himself. If for no other reason, this scene will survive at least as a reminder to future Hungarian choreographers of all that Harangozó bequeathed to the art of ballet throughout the world.

Making the rounds of the exhibition, we have come to the end of the "Harangozó room", and now, as we sum up what we have seen, glancing back for a moment before moving on to the next section, we become aware of the tremendously wide range of his achievement. Harangozó's contribution to ballet was to fuse the advances made in our own century with the newly discovered body of folk art, thus enriching the Hungarian tradition. In so doing he gave us a varied selection of works, for the most part light and carefree in character, creations that reflect his own robust artistic personality. It was a contribution that made it possible for Hungarian ballet to be recognized as equal to the finest ballet of the twentieth century, a successful combination of contemporary trends and national tradition. Harangozó launched a new era in the development of modern Hungarian ballet. And now we come to the question of future developments which will be discussed in conjunction with other aspects of the repertoire of the Budapest Ballet.

1

6–8

9–11

12–14

18–20

21–23

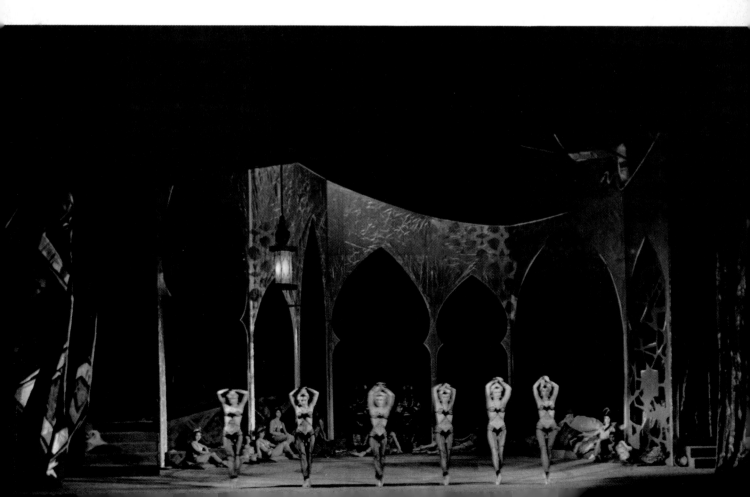

24, 25

26

THE CLASSICAL HERITAGE—BALLETS BY FOREIGN MASTERS

The development of one particular branch of art does not always run parallel to the general development of any one nation, and it frequently happens that innovations in art are absorbed into the artistic life of another country before they have been accepted in the country of their origin.

This trend is to be observed when we consider the varying stages of choreographic development of the works included in the repertoire of the Budapest Ballet. This is why it would be inappropriate to continue describing various premières in chronological order. The fact is that in the next "room" of our choreographical gallery, the visitor will find references to choreographers (and their works) who either lived before Harangozó or were working at the same time as he, though in different styles. Mikhail Fokine, the most important figure in the history of the revival of ballet in the twentieth century, enriched the repertoire of the Budapest Ballet with three works, not one of which was produced until the 1960s and even then the company was rehearsed and directed by famous Soviet choreographers. Here the skein of history is tangled indeed, for the *Chopiniana* and Stravinsky's *Firebird* and *Petrouchka* were widely produced abroad before they were seen in Hungary, and these productions in fact helped to shape the development of Hungarian Ballet.

Fokine's method was to concentrate on the authenticity of his productions. They were based on a sound knowledge of history and a serious psychological study of the characters and the national background; he was very careful to co-ordinate plot, music and scenery. This is clearly discernible in his two folk-inspired dance plays, and it was Fokine's attitude that was responsible for the new emphasis placed on dance-drama in twentieth-century developments in the art of ballet. Fokine's theories and the ballets he created had a decisive influence on Harangozó's own creative work and through this on the development of modern Hungarian ballett. Nevertheless there was a considerable time-lag between Fokine's activity as a choreographer and the presentation of his works in Hungary. This delay was made even longer by the fact that between the wars Soviet ballet had advanced rapidly, developing a style which emphasized the historical and dramatic aspects of the art while at the same time satisfying national pride. The best productions of the period were therefore produced in Hungary before the works of Fokine.

It was thus due to the strange irony and dialectics of history that long-delayed though the première was, Fokine's *Chopiniana*, an example of the new romanticism which set the course for future developments, arrived at last in Budapest at a most auspicious time. For the impact of this new romantic style on the established trends of Soviet ballet was to be of great significance.

Fokine's romantic dance-suite, ethereal, poetic and without a plot of any kind, was conceived in the classical idiom and demands a high degree of classical dancing skill, a highly polished style and the ability to communicate the pure poetry of dancing; thus it prepared the way for the symphonic ballet.

Such qualities had not been seen in Budapest in the period prior to Harangozó, nor were they developed during the new era he helped to inaugurate. The choreographic tradition at the Hungarian Opera House was neither classical nor romantic, and this was of course reflected in the place assigned to classical dancing and the standard of the dancing.

Thus, as we continue our way through the "gallery" of Hungarian choreography, we find that Fokine's ballets are located in a corridor between two sections. His works are not "displayed" in the first hall of the exhibition, but in the corridor leading from the "Harangozó room" to the "rooms" set aside for works in the romantic tradition of the nineteenth century and in the tradition of Soviet ballet between the two world wars, for all these various works serve as an introduction to present-day Hungarian ballet. At the same time we can see that Fokine's works lead naturally to the symphonic trends which are so marked a feature of the art of ballet at the present time.

It was between 1950 and 1967 that the basic works created in a nineteenth-century tradition were mastered by Hungarian ballet companies. The serpentine course of the history of ballet in our country has resulted in the appearance of later tendencies before those of an earlier date. This does not lessen their significance; in fact their tardy arrival was in itself significant because the impact coincided with similar trends in other countries.

The history of ballet during the last few years and the state of ballet at the present time shows us that it has been in countries with a living tradition of classical ballet that the standard of achievement has been highest (USSR, France). Similar standards have also been achieved where the new national ballet companies have shown simultaneously three different tendencies in their development—the revival of national traditions, the acceptance of contemporary innovations (which involved some criticism of traditional styles) and the creation of new works and a new repertoire (Great Britain, USA).

It can readily be seen, therefore, that the revival of ballet in Hungary was by no means contemporaneous with the introduction of classical traditions in choreography. The dancers also developed a technique and a style suitable for particular productions.

These productions were by no means undemanding. In fact the excellence of the repertoire mentioned above was reached and maintained only because the dancers were artists of outstanding talent who rose to the challenge of difficult works. The presence of so many gifted dancers in the company was a happy chance which coincided with Harangozó's interest in the romantic style and the arrival of Ferenc Nádasi as ballet master.

Ever since the nineteenth century, Hungarian ballet had been greatly influenced by Italian teaching methods, and a long succession of ballet masters had been invited to the Opera from Italy. Of those, Nicolas Guerra was the last to exert an exceptional influence during his activity here from 1902 to 1914. He taught a concentrated version of the Blasis School tradition which had systematized the motifs and techniques of the romantic style. Guerra trained excellent dancers and under his guidance the company as a whole attained a very high standard. He it was who launched Ferenc Nádasi, the most outstanding personality in the field of ballet training we have yet seen in Hungary. Nádasi began his studies under Guerra, and then he continued in Petersburg under Cecchetti, the great ballet master who trained Pavlova, Karsavina and Nijinsky. For more than a quarter of a century he made a career as a dancer, acclaimed by audiences throughout Europe; and all this while, Nádasi was familiarizing himself with the methods used by all the better-known ballet schools and instructors. To these he added his own unique contribution as an artist, as well as the fruits of many years of experience as a dancer and so developed the Nádasi system, which is now widely recognized and which is the basis of ballet teaching in Hungary today. Nádasi came to the Hungarian Opera House as a ballet master during the season 1937–38, and it was not long before he had trained a number of first-class soloists and had created a superb *corps de ballet* capable of fulfilling the most difficult artistic assignments, and with a general background of knowledge and skill that enabled them to develop along a number of different lines. From this time on the sureness, agility, and virtuosity of the Italian school became fused with other qualities so that the dancers were able to meet the requirements of the Harangozó style—wich demanded good acting ability, a marked display of temperament and character. This synthesis brought into being and fostered the development of a national style in the Budapest Ballet.

Nevertheless, it was not until after the war that the Budapest Ballet began to perform classical ballets conceived in the romantic tradition, and the great classical masterpieces and *études*. As we have explained, this particular style of ballet was not included in the repertoire; it was in fact unknown in Hungarian ballet generally—but this state of affairs did not last for long. For the season 1949–50 the management of the Opera invited a number of famous Soviet artists to visit Budapest, and with their coming there began a new phase in the development of Hungarian ballet. The masterpieces created in the romantic tradition of the nineteenth century which were still flourishing in the USSR, where some of them had actually originated, were now absorbed into the mainstream of Hungarian ballet. Certain works became firmly established in the repertoire, for instance the ever popular dance-plays which were the joint creations of Tchaikovsky and Petipa, and *Giselle*, which is similarly stamped with the personality of Petipa. The full-length ballets have much in common: romantic music and romantic plots, the presence of both realistic and supernatural elements, and always the beauty, magic and poetry of true love. The solos and duets of the ballet are imbued with the magic of this world and the emotions of the heroes and heroines. Around these central characters we see swans and fairies, human beings, the sons and daughters of exotic peoples and gems which assume living qualities and begin to dance—every creature imagined in fairy-tale or fable, however vivid or evanescent. This strange world of the imagination and all its colourful inhabitants illuminate the whole range of nineteenth-century ballet, it is found in both classical and character dances, and gives every opportunity to the dancers to demonstrate their skill as dancers as well as their acting ability.

Within the limited framework of this world of fantasy and poetry, these masterpieces exhibit a great deal of variety, and by their differences they complement each other. The *Nutcracker* shows us the dream-like fairy-tale world which exists in the imagination of children, a miraculous world in wich events are given special poignancy by the mood of Christmas Eve, while the realistic charachters are transformed and beautified, seen through the spellbound eyes of the young people. The ballet is imbued with the luminous atmosphere of simple beauty and innocence as apprehended in the imagination of a child.

The theme of *Swan Lake* is more complex than anything found in a fairy-tale. Here true love must find the strength to break the spell cast by an evil wizard. This monster has in his power the young girls who have been captured and changed into swans and it is their melancholy and bitter-sweet emotions that dominate the beautiful group dances in the great "white" acts. The power of his own love enables the young prince to release the snow-white swan-maiden from the evil spell, and love is seen to triumph over sorcery and the forces of destruction.

Giselle is also a a joyful and poetic work concerned with the triumph of love, but this time only beyond the grave; for Giselle is too frail to survive the disappointments of this world. Her death is due to the irresponsibility, rashness and deceitfulness of the Duke, and by all the rules recognized in the world of fairy-tales, this early death calls for revenge. Giselle's pure love, however, breaks through this ruthless tradition and frail though she is, she has the nobility to forgive the man who destroyed her and whom she loved so deeply, and to obtain for him life in the next world.

The theme of romantic love is interwoven into every one of these immortal ballets; we see the triumph of love, its poignancy and the happiness it brings, and the emotional content of these works, and their poetic qualities, continue to enchant the audiences of our own harassed times. Here we are shown a world so remote from our experience, where all is harmony and beauty, that nowadays we are scarcely affected by the actual story. But the plot is sustained, carried forward and given substance by the magic of classical dancing, and we forget its naiveté as we succumb to the beauty of the dancing.

In *The Sleeping Beauty* too it is the harmony and purity of the classical dancing, the very essence of beauty as found in the art of ballet, that enchants the audiences of today. Here the plot is so slight and loosely woven that it scarcely even serves to connect the brilliant series of dances that accompany the harmonies and rhythmic music of Tchaikovsky. Each dance is a gem in itself, sparkling evidence of Petipa's unparalleled musicality and spectacular manner of composition, his brilliant inventiveness and skill as a choreographer. Nevertheless, when compared to the earlier ballets, this dance-play seems remote, coolly detached and abstract. Romance, plot and emotional extravagance give way to a poeticism that is more universal, a quality of restraint that already foreshadows a twentieth-century style and the emergence of the symphonic ballet mentioned in connection with the *Chopiniana*.

It is then a romantic poeticism and nobility of outlooks, as well as the pure classical dancing, that links these ballets. These are the qualities offered to audiences and these are the qualities demanded of the dancers, both soloists and chorus. The works demand such qualities and at the same time foster them; the inclusion of these works in the repertoire of any company indicates that the standard of both teaching and dancing is of a high order, as in the case of the Budapest Ballet.

These works made use of every skill acquired by the company as a result of Nádasi's brilliant teaching and thus they too helped to improve the standard of the company. The dancers re-learned the principles of classical ballet, this time reaching an even higher standard of technique and especially of style; at the same time they absorbed all those modifications of the tradition made by the great Soviet masters— V. Vainonen, A. Messerer, L. Lavrovsky, and P. Gusev—modifications demonstrated by the great Soviet companies in the theatres of Moscow and Leningrad.

It is a well-known fact that wherever tradition is cherished, whether by individual artists, teachers, even schools, and particularly by companies and theatres, there also we find some new contribution to the tradition. This explains the fact that the standard works of ballet are never danced in exactly the same way everywhere; there is always some slight difference in the interpretation and emphasis at every performance. In all these developments the Bolshoi Theatre of Moscow was an example to the Budapest Ballet. The essential features of this style are emotional poignancy and dramatic significance: every movement is charged with feeling and the dancing is always powerfully expressive, though of course adapted in measure and manner to suit the individual needs of any one ballet. This is the basis of the lyricism, beauty, harmony and plasticity of movement achieved by the company, and this also explains the dynamism and virtuosity of the dancing. Similar definitions have been given by a number of English, French and American experts—each working in a somewhat different style—when they contrasted the Bolshoi style with their own work. Scarcely less important than this emotional fervour and poignancy of style is the dramatic quality which led to such splendid artistic achievements in the principal works of the Soviet ballet in the period between the two world wars.

When speaking of Fokine, we have already mentioned that his works led to developments in two directions, to the symphonic ballet and to the dramatic ballet. The Soviet ballets composed between 1930 and 1940 which found a place in the repertoire of the Budapest Ballet were in the dramatic style. These works satisfy Fokine's demand for dramatic authenticity and complexity as expressed in the historical and psychological reality of the character portrayal and plot development, its genuine national and folk character, and the full dramatic integration of plot, music, dance and scenery, and they also incorporate the tradition of the romantic ballet in several acts. At the same time these works demonstrate a vigorous striving to combine various idioms of dancing—classical, folk art and pantomime—and an insistance on the part of the director of a well-planned dramatic structure. This concept and style was gradually accepted in Hungary during the 1950s, and was absorbed into the current developments together and parallel with the nineteenth-century classical tradition. These works therefore had a decisive influence on the style, manner and trends of Hungarian ballet and a corresponding effect on the taste and preferences shown by Hungarian audiences.

The four ballets which the Budapest Ballet produced within a single decade and which still have a significant place in the repertoire, exemplify the unique qualities of Soviet ballet dating from the great period of the nineteen-thirties.

The Flames of Paris is the oldest of them. In it, Soviet ballet, through the direct agency of Vainonen, astonished the world by staging the very apotheosis of a people in revolution. True choreographic genius is shown in this work and particularly in the third act when the different stylized French folk dances seen side by side become gradually imbued with the militant spirit of revolution as the people prepare themselves in body and soul for the uprising; the dances assume an unequivocally dramatic function, helping to build up the unforgettable climax when the masses rise up in revolt; here is a style of choreography that serves as a model from now on for every new dance creation with a similar theme. On the other hand, the festive *divertissement* in the fourth act, something of an appendix, is a display of classical solo dancing and a great test for the star soloists of any company.

The Fountain of Bakhchisarai (music by Boris Asafiev who also composed the music for *The Flames of Paris*) is a version for ballet of the dramatic poem by Pushkin. In the first act of the work Zakharov, the choreographer-director, provided a masterly exposition of the drama in dances inspired by Pushkin's own lines; but in the third act an extremely tense and dramatic dialogue was given a highly satisfactory choreographic formulation. The harem scene in the second act, and later the magnificent Mongolian dances in Act Four, prepare and close, respectively, the portrayal of character and development of the plot. It may be seen therefore that the work has many virtues to recommend it to audiences: it is a highly concentrated dance-drama which makes exacting demands on the performers both as dancers and as actors.

Aram Khachaturian's splendid, colourfully oriental ballet *Gayane* was rehearsed in Budapest by the first choreographer to design this work, Anisimova. Later, in 1967, the company revived this piece in the form of a suite, which smoothly unites classical technique of a high order with a series of character dances inspired by folk art. Thus, although the libretto is rather confusing, the work contains many successful dances, including the picturesque and stirring character dances, which enable the company to display all the commendable virtues associated with its name ever since the early period of Harangozó's activity.

The repertoire of the Budapest Ballet includes Lavrovsky's version of Sergei Prokofiev's *Romeo and Juliet*, which represents all that is best in the Soviet dance-dramas, a work which will undoubtedly become one of the great classics of the future. The dancing is infused with the poetry and drama of the Shakespearian play and the whole ballet permeated with the beauty of each separate art. In this work we find some of the greatest individual scenes and dances in modern ballet: the scene when the lovers first meet, the wedding, the duels, Mercutio's death, the farewell after the wedding-night, the scene in which Juliet, almost paralyzed with grief, dances with Paris after Romeo's departure, the scene in which she takes leave of life, and the final scene in the crypt when Romeo dances the "duet" with a Juliet from whom life has departed.

There are also many fine character dances, each one of them beautifully timed in the dramatic sequence —but it is probably unnecessary to demonstrate still further the fact that in this work the dancing and the acting are fused at the highest level of artistic achievement, outstanding achievement even by Soviet ballet standards. The dance drama is a challenge to the most gifted of solo artists and enables them to reach a pinnacle of achievement hitherto unknown in the art of choreography. It is a style that encompasses classical and folk dancing, traditional group dancing and pantomime, while the art of acting and of fencing is seen in dancing of the very highest order; the artistic form of this work is essentially that of dancing, an art which is here so creative that it may perhaps even add something to the original play by Shakespeare.

The dancers of the Budapest Ballet company incorporated in their productions of the Soviet ballets mentioned above the finest traditions of romantic and classical dancing as demonstrated in their performances of the folk and character dances in those works; but they reached an equally high standard in their interpretation of the dance-drama in *Romeo and Juliet*.

Throughout the present century Fokine, like other creative and original artists in this field, was deeply concerned with the art of music and especially of music for the ballet, with and without a plot, whether specially composed for the stage or adapted to meet the requirements of production. From this renewed interest in music there emerged what is perhaps one of the most important features of modern ballet: a more discriminating choice of music for the ballet and the use of music not originally intended for the ballet.

Fokine himself had already designed ballets for compositions which existed in their own right as works of art, for instance, his *Chopiniana*, *The Dying Swan* and *Sheherazade*. Isadora Duncan, Émile Jacques-Dalcroze and Rudolf Laban, those celebrated pioneers of expressive dancing, sometimes known as 'modern' dancing, also chose freely from the music of the world for their ballet compositions, with the intention of expressing that music on the stage.

After the nineteen-thirties, the period dominated by the dramas of the Russian Ballet, the chief concern of Western choreography (including contemporary Hungarian ballet) was the expression through dancing of a number of symphonic works. This was the case particularly with those choreographers who were naturally sensitive to music and who were able to subordinate their ideas of dance composition to the inspiration of the music.

Among these choreographers were the former associates of Diaghilev—Bronislava Nijinska, Leonide Massine, and especially Georges Balanchine, who remains to this day the most eminent of them all. The works created by these great artists foreshadowed the emergence of symphonic ballet, the characteristic style of contemporary ballet.

As early as in 1931 experiments had been made in this style by a Pole, Jan Cieplinski, an ex-member of the Diaghilev and Pavlova companies, who had worked as a choreographer in Hungary prior to Harangozó and also in the nineteen-forties contemporaneously with him. He composed a plotless ballet based on Glasunov's *The Seasons* in which the essence of the music was expressed in the poetry of movement, but this innovation met with no response and was not developed by anyone else.

Harangozó's interest is essentially in the dramatic aspects of the art, so he did not even attempt to compose this kind of ballet; in any case, as we have seen, the nineteen-fifties were dominated by the dramatic style of ballet which for a time excluded all others at the Budapest Opera House. Perhaps this concentration in one single style was necessary at that time to allow for the consolidation of past achievements; but the addition of some works of symphonic ballet would certainly have enriched the repertoire. Sooner or later the demand for this style was bound to arise in Hungary, too, the more so as the range of music to be heard in the nineteen-fifties became so restricted.

Yet the best interests of the Opera, home of the Budapest Ballet, are served by offering to the public the widest possible repertoire. Cieplinski's choreographical works are a notable contribution to theatrical tradition: it is just because of their musicality and high culture that the repertoire still includes two of his works, the adaptation of Ravel's *Bolero*, and the great dance in the opera the *Queen of Sheba* by the Hungarian composer, Károly Goldmark.

Musical invention, sensitivity to style and effective spectacle are characteristic of both these works, with the dance following the internal movement, the melodic and rhythmic articulation and structure of the music as well as the richly modulated orchestration. The dancing is made to serve the music with humility though always seeking a high standard of its own; and the dancers are given opportunities of moving and breathing to the very pulse and changing mood of the music while yet enriching it with their own art.

But Cieplinski deserves to be mentioned not only for his musicality, but also because of his choreographic style. His experience of the art of dancing was both extensive and intensive and he showed an excellent sense of style in his handling of different types of dances, chiefly Spanish and Oriental. In some of his other works, now no longer performed, he adhered to the Expressionist style, a trend which was not followed up for some time.

Internationally, however, new developments were taking place in the symphonic style of ballet and in the Expressionist style, and it was inevitable that in the end these developments should be made known in Hungary and absorbed into Hungarian ballet. Jazz dancing, which had been internationally acclaimed for several decades, also had to be accepted at the Budapest Opera, not only to satisfy public demand but also as a necessary stage in the development of the art of dancing in Hungary.

During the nineteen-sixties there emerged a number of new Hungarian choreographers with the talent necessary to meet these new demands.

28–32

33, 34

35, 36

37, 38

39–41

42, 43

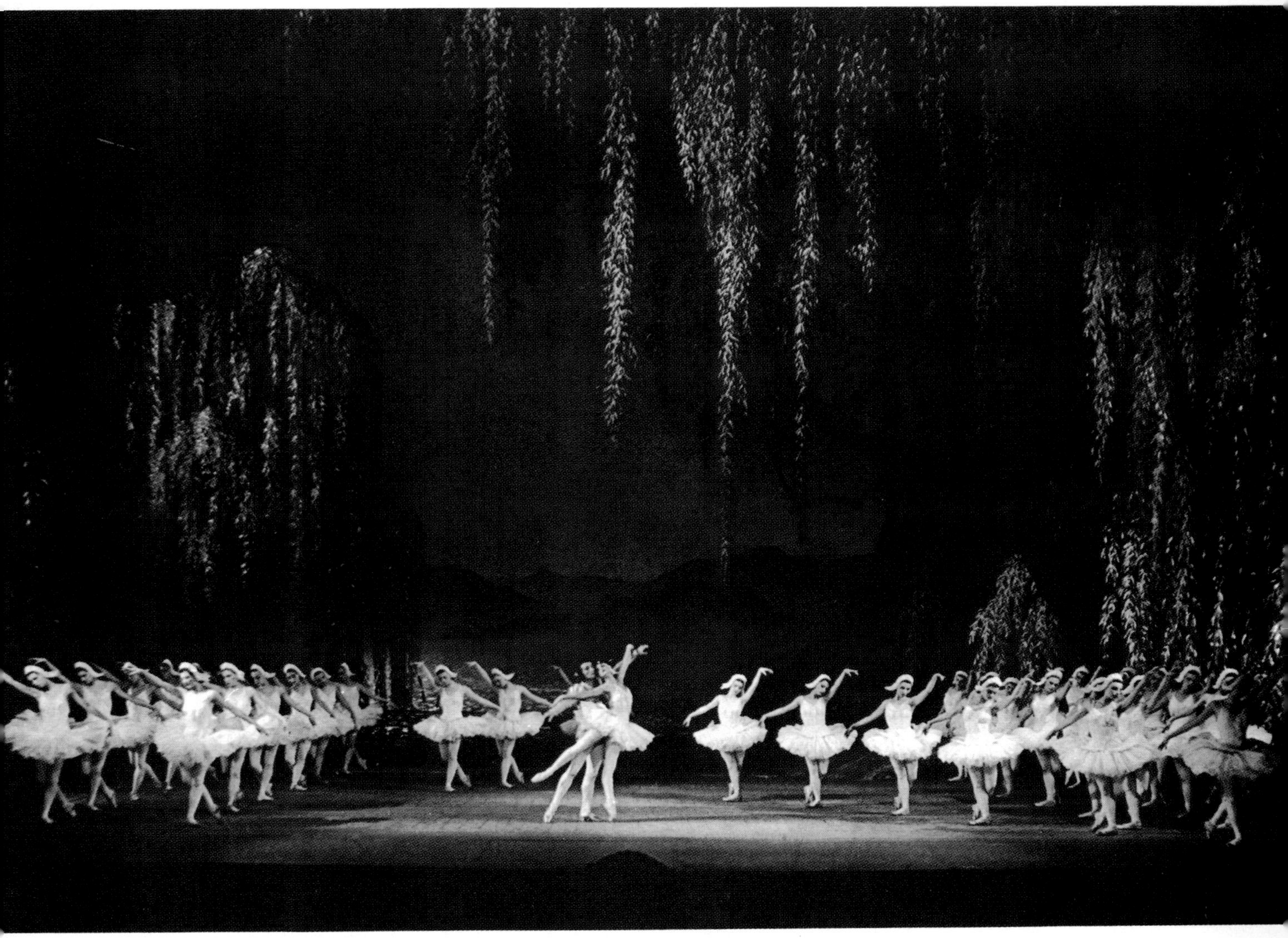

44, 45

46, 47

53, 54

55, 56

59, 60

61, 62

63, 64

65, 66

71, 72

73, 74

75–77

NEW HUNGARIAN CHOREOGRAPHIES

It is to *Imre Eck* that we must give most of the credit for building up a new repertoire. His name is widely known in Hungary and abroad; it is usually mentioned in connection with the Ballet Sopianae of the university city of Pécs in south-west Hungary. He founded and trained this company, and his own original work was closely bound up with its development; indirectly, through the medium of the Ballet Sopianae, he influenced the Budapest Ballet company.

Imre Eck began as a dancer with the Budapest Ballet and first worked as a choreographer in the early nineteen-fifties. His shorter works and individual dances for concerts were first performed by members of the ballet company at some of their performances at concerts or in variety programmes. He received his first independent commission from the Opera in 1959, when he was asked to produce with the Budapest company the romantic Hungarian fairy-tale *Csongor and Tünde*, with music by Leo Weiner; this had been produced some decades earlier by Cieplinski, but it had not been included in the repertoire for many years. This was a work well suited to Eck's talent as a choreographer and he found ingenious ways of expressing the characters, evil, shrewd and comic, of the hero and heroine's enemies (the witch, her daughter, and the devilkins). Moreover this work, the first of Eck's large projects, contained elements of the gymnastic and acrobatic movement and the frieze-like architectural composition for which he became famous.

His characteristic and original talent was, however, more evident in his previous creation, the great ballet inserted in Gluck's opera *Orpheus* (1958). But his true contribution to the art of choreography could not be given full expression in the Gluck opera where his own work was but a small part of the whole, restricted of necessity by the style and dramatic structure of the opera. His art did not fully develop until he began his work with the Ballet Sopianae two years later; this marked the beginning of a continuous period of highly productive choreographic activity.

Eck made his début as a choreographer with a highly characteristic work, *Orpheus*, which is still included in the company's repertoire and is frequently performed today. In content, approach, idiom and style this work is original, as are all his works; and as always, the choreography is closely dependent on the music.

We see here a philosophical attitude, visionary and tormented, an interest in gestures, poses and tableaux; a knowledge of classical dancing, but a deliberate turning away from its traditional language and aesthetics towards expressive dancing. All these elements appeared in the *Orpheus* ballet, anticipating important features of the choreographic style which matured at Pécs.

When the Budapest Opera again invited Imre Eck to prepare a choreography, he was already well known as the designer of several choreographies which had been well received by the public. Most of them were designed for works by contemporary Hungarian composers and the choreographic approach was essentially similar to that of his previous works, but the early tendencies had now developed and matured. It was essentially a philosophical approach, with a deliberate striving for, and acceptance of, intellectualism; in all his works Imre Eck explored with feverish intensity both public and private problems of contemporary life as well as those experienced in recent history, but his work also shows a certain emotional dryness and reserve interestingly combined with vigorous eroticism and open sexuality. This same intonation, outlook and style may be observed in his ballet versions of Stravinsky's *Le Sacre du Printemps*, Ravel's *Daphnis and Chloe*, and Bartók's *Music for Strings, Percussion and Celesta*.

These three works have been of great significance in the development of twentieth-century music and ballet. Today it is almost obligatory to include the Stravinsky ballet in the repertoire of any company that calls itself modern, for Stravinsky marks the highest achievements in the sphere of ballet music. It can be said that the *Sacre* marked a turning point even in the varied and dialectically exciting developments of contemporary music. This work, with its barbaric rhythmic and tonal patterns, expressing a total musical exaltation, opened the way for still newer developments, something agonizingly modern that can suggest and formulate the growing harassment of a world in which mysterious and evil forces are at work.

Ravel approached his theme with a contemporary sense of nostalgia for the past and therefore presented us with a powerfully poetic and sublimated view of antiquity. His work is impressionistic, an orgy of brightly coloured sounds, and its gossamer-like poeticism transports artists and spectators alike into the world of neo-Classicism.

Eck's conception and production of *Le Sacre du Printemps* provoked much lively discussion in Hungarian music circles, for the choreographer fitted to the music new ideas or "action", basically different from the mood of the original work. In opposition to the notes and the score, the dancing conveys Eck's subjective ideas about the origin of man, the evolution of the world from chaos, the inorganic and later the organic world; and this vision is presented against a background of continual strife, struggle and danger, so that Eck also suggests the basic insecurity of the present age and hints that this is man's most fundamental problem in all ages. The final effect of the work is to show that this philosophical approach to the problem of choreography is not a contradiction of the music; in fact this combination is seen to be a possible way of interpreting the Stravinsky composition for the stage.

Of course, the manner in which Eck handled the music in this work is again characteristic of his personal attitude as an artist. Like other contemporary choreographers—of whom Maurice Béjart was perhaps the first—he undertakes the task of rewriting ballets with a definite subject, and daringly interprets various original symphonic works, chiefly Baroque or twentieth-century, in his own subjective idiom. This is an artistic approach that has more than once produced astonishing choreographies with a message significantly different and sometimes even contrary to the generally accepted interpretation of the original work, and those who criticize his art are no less passionate in their views than his admirers.

In his ballet version of *Daphnis and Chloe*, Eck respected Fokine's libretto as much as possible, designing for it a new, neo-classical choreography in which he stressed the modern quality of Ravel's work by introducing movements and poses typical of his own art. The choreography is convincing in its mood and the long dance duets are particularly successful. Although the choreographer apparently ran out of energy to cope really well with the rousing baccchanalia that closes the music and the action, still, this adaptation is unusually successful in that it solves the problem of bringing to the stage a work

96

based on wonderful music, and handles adequately all those symphonic characteristics which would seem to have predestined this composition for the concert platform rather than the ballet stage.

Of all the ballets Eck designed for the Opera, Bartók's *Music* is the most significant, although compared with the two earlier pieces, this work posed many more objective difficulties. The *Music for Strings, Percussion and Celesta* is an intrinsically musical work presenting a complete and closed world in itself, a superb example of Bartók's genius. This work provides a key to the understanding of Bartók's mature art, for it is a condensed and sharply stated summary of the mature period and at the same time of the human and artistic problems with which the composer was at that time concerned. It is the epitome of everything the composer absorbed and assimilated from twentieth-century music and the folk music of centuries past only to re-formulate it with his own incomparable genius, using musical themes, intonation and rhythm, structure and design to create new works.

Eck's choreography expresses the philosophical and emotional reverberations of Bartók's composition, the tension that lies at the heart of it, the conflict and the final resolution. There is then no "action" except insofar as the dancers express the momentum of the music by the more direct and concrete means of spectacle, movement and movement compositions.

The heroes of the work are a human couple and a group. The couple in fact represents Man, a unity of man and woman, and the group (consisting of twelve female dancers) represents sometimes the environment that surrounds and opposes man, and sometimes the counter-poles of human intellect and emotion, man's inner conflicts and difficulties. These symbolic figures are shown within a choreographic conception of man as a being capable of belief and doubt, desire and self-denial, rebellion and resignation; to put it another way, he shows that man, capable as he is of thought and feeling, is engaged in a continuous and exhausting struggle, whether he likes it or not, with his environment and with himself; he must accept this strife, he wages the struggle and triumphs.

In creating his designs for the Bartók work Eck showed himself to have a hand that was both talented and lucky. He was able to pick out a possible and essential conception from the almost inexhaustible richness of the music and essentially he solved the very difficult task he had set for himself. In his choreography the human couple were made aesthetically convincing through the classical style and the eloquence of their movements; the portrayal of the group in Eck's individual idiom, in the third movement, is particularly expressive, vigorous and dramatic.

The music of Bartók and symphonic dancing seem to belong naturally to the world of Hungarian ballet; here is some mutual attraction that can be readily explained and appreciated. It was inevitable that the art of ballet in Hungary and the Opera itself, which was the leading theatre in the sphere of music, should have received a tremendous stimulus from the new possibility of interpreting Bartók for the stage; after the creation of these two ballets, there was an intense desire to express through the art of dancing his symphonic works.

This tremendous interest in Bartók was due not only to an awareness of his greatness as a composer but also to the intrinsically motorial character of his compositions which seem to ask for dance and movement.

A version for ballet of the orchestral work entitled *Dance Suite* was produced as early as in 1948 when Harangozó created for the stage a work full of incident, as much a play as a ballet, after Béla Balázs's libretto. This version had but a short life in the repertoire, but the challenge of putting the *Suite* on the stage inspired another attempt in due course, this time in the form of a symphonic ballet, a form certainly better suited to the character of the musical composition.

Sándor Barkóczy's choreography for the *Dance Suite* was more successful in a variety of ways. The choreography is musically sensitive, faithfully and flexibly following the fluctuations in the mood of the music, its structure and design, its characteristic motifs, and exciting, vibrant rhythm. The confronting of the different movements raises dramatic problems without solving them, but the effective and expressive solo parts, and especially some of the male group dances with their folk-music intonation (here Barkóczy showed a particular flair), express the very essence of the music which is so closely connected with the tradition of folk music.

In this work Barkóczy utilized simultaneously the motifs and possibilities of classical dancing, stylized folk dancing and sometimes even purely expressive gestures and poses. His style of choreography might well be described as a kind of national neo-Classicism.

This is the world of movement which attracts and interests Barkóczy, a talented choreographer who studied in Moscow. His splendid professionalism is also demonstrated in another, earlier work, his choreography for Prokofiev's *Classical Symphony*.

Barkóczy was truly inspired by Prokofiev's music and he was able to create a symphonic ballet which translates into the art of dancing a contemporary work which was written in the pure classical style, a ballet which is quite devoid of action, either external or internal. As a spectacle it is artistically pleasing, the music and the dancing are both of a high standard, the general conception is lucid and Barkóczy shows an ability to use the classical language of movement in an ambitious and ingenious manner. The solo and the duet are excellent, and he is equally successful with the spatial arrangement of the group dances, and the way in which he breaks them up, particularly in the second and third movements. It is therefore hardly surprising to find that this work has become one of the most successful neo-classical symphonic pieces in the repertoire.

There can be no doubt that one method of approach which is still acceptable to choreographers today is that which involves the rewriting of a given composition to meet the requirements of dancing and spectacle: in this approach the choreographer's imagination is freely inspired by the music. Meaning is never conveyed through action—which tends to modify both music and dancing—and this kind of dancing devoid of concrete dramatic significance seems to be able to come close to the essence of music. This is its great attraction, for in this way an infinite realm of music has become available for dancers who are by temperament particularly susceptible to the poetic aspects of dancing, the world of "pure dancing" as opposed to that of the dance-drama.

Because dancing is such a many-sided art, throughout the history of the ballet there have been creative artists whose approach emphasized one aspect of the art—the music, the dramatic possibilities or the relationship between ballet and the fine arts. This is also true of Hungarian ballet. Gyula Harangozó, for instance, finds it natural to create in the spirit of the drama, of the play with a plot; Imre Eck's works are dominated by the plastic and architectonic elements—those aspects of the art of dancing which came closest to the fine arts, whereas Sándor Barkóczy and the young *László Seregi* represent the type of choreographer whose primary response is to the music.

Music, dance, spectacle—all may now be seen in Seregi's choreographies at the Opera House, where he is now attaining new heights in a career which began with the Dance and Song Ensemble of the

People's Army, where he was both dancer and choreographer, interested chiefly in the technique of ballet combined with acrobatics. In the late nineteen-fifties Seregi was already one of the leading character dancers at the Opera House, working as a free-lance choreographer for the theatre and for television. Since 1961 he has regularly been commissioned to design the choreography for the new productions of various operas in widely differing styles. He also designed the choreography for the jazz-ballet in the first Hungarian dance film, to be made as a full-length three-part feature.

The short ballets for opera mentioned above are always of a strictly defined character and are a challenge to the skill of any choreographer: they may be described as a training and testing ground for members of this profession. Seregi showed considerable talent in making good use of his opportunities, and his short ballets for opera, about one act in length, were all well received—Millöcker's *The Beggar Student*, Rossini's *William Tell*, Kozma's *Electronic Love*, Orff's *The Clever Girl*, Kodály's *Spinning-Room*, Gounod's *Faust*, Wagner's *Tannhäuser*, Strauss's *Die Fledermaus*. His works are a living part of the repertoire of the Budapest Ballet (and are sometimes shown without a supporting programme). They are often performed by the Budapest Ballet and they always give the impression that they have been created by an outstanding choreographer.

We can only mention a few of his works in these pages—those which, in their individuality and in their style, are most characteristic as expressions of Seregi's creative virtuosity. *The Beggar Student* remains memorable as his first work of this kind, especially as the classical and character dances, the quality of the music, sense of style, idiomatic inventiveness and sure sense of design indicate that he was already a mature artist.

The dance scenes of *Spinning-Room* demand a good knowledge of folk music. In this work Seregi was able to draw on his folk-dancing background to good effect. Concisely—with a few well-selected movements—he manages to characterize several different types, and to create a powerful ballad-like atmosphere. His dances are ethnically authentic and dramatically well placed. In this work Seregi introduced to the Opera a type of ballet directly influenced by Hungarian folk dancing.

While working on the *Spinning-Room* Seregi was almost simultaneously designing the choreography for the modern part of the Hungarian dance film entitled *The Girl Danced into Life*, in which the plot and dances are set in present-day Budapest. It is a film version of a Hungarian folk ballad in which the heroine, *The Girl Danced into Death*, is presented in various periods of history; but in the present-day setting there is a hopeful ending to what was formerly a tragedy. Among the effective jazz dances in the modern scenes there is a great love duet, a popular offering when members of the company are asked to perform at concerts. This is a well-designed choreography with an ambitious use of motif and a skilful and effective blending of the elements of ballet and jazz; it is also deeply musical, a convincing *tour de force*, born of Seregi's wide range of knowledge and his interest in modern art.

The *Valpurgis Night* scene in the opera *Faust* is regarded as one of the gems of romantic ballet music, a fact which facilitates the task of the modern choreographer while at the same time presenting him with certain difficulties. The romantic style of this well-known music and the mythological convention attached to it have a restricting influence on a creative artist, while the lilting melodies themselves produce almost the effect of movement and dancing. On the other hand, any ambitious and modern director of opera would certainly feel that this romanticism must be conveyed differently nowadays, that a successful production must be in the spirit of the modern dance and modern spectacle. Seregi managed to do justice to this artistic challenge too when he used the original six scenes of the ballet to create a unified but flowing work full of colour and variety, with neither concrete setting nor figures, he built up, in harmony with the dramatic movement of the music, following its melodic, dynamic and rhythmic texture, a spectacular series of dance tableaux in which the solo, the *pas de deux*, and the group dances are shaped according to the degree of their eroticism. Particularly successful is the dance of the virtuous but unruly fauns; also the wildly erotic "golden duet", the splendid water scene produced in shades of blue and silver, and the crimson glow of the sophisticated finale; these scenes give members of the company every opportunity to demonstrate their advanced technique.

The *Venus Cave* scene in *Tannhäuser* presented a similar dramatic problem, although the nature of the music and the function of the dances is in this case much more restricted and purposeful. Here the cosmic dimensions, the almost crippling power of passionate physical love has to be expressed by faithfully following and capturing the magic of the mighty waves of Wagner's music. Seregi's choreography manages to turn every mood and form in this music, so reminiscent of the eternal tides of the sea, into a flowing spectacle of movement. His choreographic idiom follows the emotional sweep of the music and thus approaches the staccato expressive style in which poses and pictures play an important part. One of the dangers of this style is that dancing is to a great extent replaced by static means of expression, with the result that there may be a break in the continuity of the movement which lasts only from pose to pose. Seregi was able to avoid this difficulty: what he created remains dancing, that is, continuous movement in which, however, sculptural tableaux also play an important part and carry, together with the movement, both artistic and dramatic significance.

These one-act ballets without dramatic plot exemplify the richness of Seregi's choreographic talent: the continuously high level of his artistic achievement, his gift for spectacle, his rich inventiveness, sensitivity to the forms of dancing, the versatility of his idiom and his great musicality. He is a choreographer who can work with a sure hand in many widely divergent styles of music and dancing.

This is no mean accomplishment and anyone who has seen his work is readily convinced that Seregi is an important master of the lyrical and the symphonic dance. It was, however, some years before the choreographer achieved a success in the genre of the independent dance-drama which poses many new and complex problems.

In the spring of 1968, however, Seregi rose to this challenge too. For his independent début Seregi chose Khachaturian's three-act ballet *Spartacus*, and having written a new text to the music—which was then suitably condensed and adapted to the new conception—he was widely acclaimed for his achievement. The reason why this ballet received a tremendous reception from Hungarian audiences was, of course, primarily due to the outstanding quality of the design, but the general effect was enhanced by additional features.

We have to remember that during the last twenty years in the history of the Budapest Ballet, Hungarian audiences—we might even say the new Hungarian audiences—have come to equate ballet primarily with the full-length dramatic dance-play in several acts; that is what they are used to and that is what they have come to appreciate. But during the nineteen-sixties the Budapest Ballet produced mainly one-act ballets, with the intention of broadening and enriching the repertoire both musically and choreographically, and to make good certain deficiencies. Great works by twentieth-century composers were brought to life on the stage through the art of ballet; but though the choreographic interpretation was generally of a high standard, these works did not appeal to audiences as did the dance-plays, so poetic, dramatic and romantic, nor yet the Soviet dance-dramas, each so rich in action and dancing.

Audiences at the Opera House were once more eager to acclaim some new ballet drama when *Spartacus* arrived to fulfill all their hopes. The ballet offers the poetry of drama and dancing combined, an ambitious theme and a pleasing spectacle; it is a work both intensely thoughtful and full of deep feeling. In *Spartacus* we have a summary of the most important achievements of the last thirty years or so in the art of dancing in Hungary. Seregi was inspired by many different styles when he created this work: the national dance-play devised by Harangozó, the Soviet ballet drama, rooted in Classicism but full of feeling, the highly expressive folk dance, modern and jazz dancing with their new forms and patterns, and the style which incorporates the flash-back and that play with time and past associations so characteristic of modern film and literature. The choreographer showed great talent and ingenuity in his use of these sources, while at the same time incorporating in the work all that was best in his own early creations. The techniques he had already tried out in earlier work he now used to portray heroes of different social status and nationality and to depict a variety of dramatic situations and moods, yet he was able to integrate these representations into a colourful ballet with a unified style.

This work was the first in the history of Hungarian ballet in which a Hungarian choreographer at the Budapest Opera brought to the stage revolution and revolutionaries. His hero, moreover, was no glorious victor in battle: he was the defeated leader of rebellious slaves, a man whose name has become a universal symbol of courageous and selfless struggle for freedom and progress.

Seregi's treatment of the theme is very interesting, sustaining throughout our awareness of the glory of struggle and revolution in spite of defeat. He constructed the plot by showing three points of view: each act represents a different phase of the story, showing the attitude to events of Spartacus, Crassus, the victorious Roman general, and Flavia, Spartacus's wife respectively, from the outbreak of the revolt until its tragic defeat.

There is a bold opening scene after which the events leading up to the outbreak of the revolt are depicted as hallucinations of the crucified Spartacus as his mind turns to the past away from his present agony. Thus we see the school for gladiators, exhausting military exercises, the parting from his beloved and all his friends, a mortal duel between friends arranged by Crassus and his cronies for their own entertainment, and finally the uprising of the slaves; these scenes make up the first act, so that the solo and group dances and the great dramatic scenes (especially the exciting duel composed in various idioms of dancing) provide for the audience a succession of thrills. Seregi also managed to create a highly individual choreography which conveyed all the rich content of Vainonen's *The Flames of Paris*. He also expressed in his choreography the way in which an oppressed people were gradually roused to the point of revolt; but though he repeats the dramatic situation in each act, the choreographic treatment of the situation is never the same.

Spartacus is seen on the cross, gazing with dimming eyes at a vision of the Appian Way lined with the bodies of crucified slaves stretching into the dim distance, while between them men who have been forced to bow their knees as slaves rise to their feet to live again, banding together with an irrepressible stream of men. It is a stirring sight, but the men are crushed by the Roman legionaries, armour-clad and bearing shields, while in their wake appears the enemy victor, Crassus.

The two scenes of the second act are separated from each other in time. In the first scene, it is some years after the revolt, and we are shown Crassus in the ruined arena of Capua trying to discover the secret of his heroic opponent's strength. The second scene takes us back to the period before the uprising, and now we are shown the feast in the garden of Crassus's summer palace, when the guests are "disturbed" by a group of liberated slaves. This act comes closest to the ballet in genre, for it is built up of a splendid series of dances in two great *divertissement*s, in the second of which we are again shown the power of the triumphant people as they break into a dance.

In the last act events are seen for the most part through the sad eyes of Flavia. This is the most deeply moving part of the work, for the great grief embodied in its sad but beautiful dances has the power to purify and uplift the human spirit. We witness the tortuous retreat of the defeated armies, the slaves taking leave of each other, the final battle and then a dark visionary scene in which the victors march on in triumph; finally we see once again the line of crosses on the Via Appia and the whole act is a tearful lament for a freedom that has been lost and lives that have been sacrificed.

And though earlier we stressed that this work constitutes a summary of all that Seregi had learned, we must now emphasize a few of the individual designs which shed new light on Seregi as a choreographer and director of genius. This is shown immediately in the opening scene of the ballet which is of astounding originality and almost shocking in the violence of its contrasting elements: the rows of crosses and the crucified hero on the one hand, and on the other, his delirious dream of the young girls he played with in his youth, sunlit figures seen dancing at his feet, graceful and ethereal.

We have already mentioned the dance which portrays the masses as they shake off their chains, creep forward on their knees through the dust and then stand up to proclaim a genuine people's revolution. And there is one other scene, superb in its emotional quality and in its choreography, that must not be left unmentioned. The gladiators chosen to take part in a duel had to spend the night in isolation, and this scene shows the four friends together for the last time. The four men dance together with Spartacus's wife who has been smuggled in to say good-bye to her husband, a dance which magnificently translates the conception of love and friendship into the poetry of movement. Of the many dances portraying the feast at Crassus's summer palace, the splendid "bell dance" deserves special notice, for in it we find a tremendous concentration of musical talent, inventiveness and the gift for visual arrangements. The last dance duet of the ballet, in which Spartacus takes leave of Flavia, is one of the most beautiful *pas de deux* in the art of contemporary dance in Hungary, a beautiful portrayal of the hero and heroine, in the most condensed terms of choreography.

79, 80

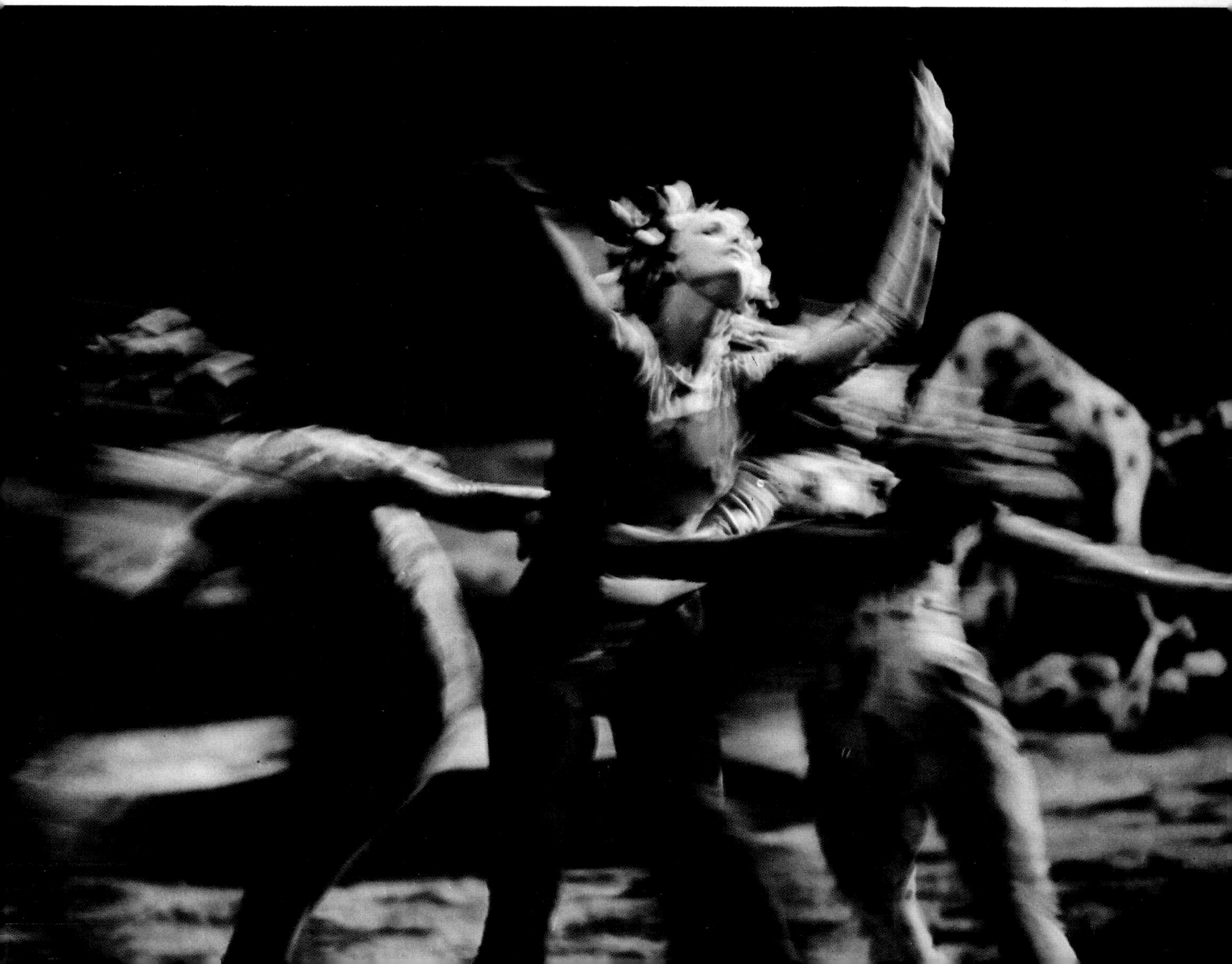

81–83

84, 85

86–88

89, 90

91, 92

93, 94

95, 96

97, 98

102–105

THE COMPANY AND ITS PRINCIPAL SOLOISTS

The full beauty and richness of the repertoire described in the foregoing chapters is, of course, conveyed to audiences only because of the high artistic standard, knowledge and dramatic ability of all the members of the company, artists, soloists and *corps de balets* alike. The Budapest Ballet company has been fortunate to acquire in the course of the last decades a host of artists with the professional knowledge and dancing skill needed for a great variety of styles and techniques, both traditional and contemporary. The company as a whole has studied and practised both classical and character dancing, neo-classical and symphonic ballet, lyric and dramatic dancing, modern dancing and jazz dancing, the music of the past and the music of our own times. New ideas were absorbed into the heritage of the past and this combined body of knowledge helped to shape the character of the ensemble as a whole and influenced the way in which they produced works in different styles. The company is therefore rich and wide-ranging in its character, rather complex but nevertheless dominated by a few unique and outstanding features. Well-known foreign experts, for instance, Olga Lepeshinskaya and Kurt Peters, editor-in-chief of the periodical *Tanzarchiv*, have declared that the performances of the Budapest Ballet are distinguished by three main qualities, those qualities which similarly distinguish Hungarian dancers, namely: that they have been very well trained technically in the classical dance, that they can convey the rich emotional content of dances in various styles, and finally that they show marked ability as actors. This comprehensive characterization makes it apparent that the most salient features of the Budapest Ballet company are best demonstrated in traditional national dances and in dance-dramas, whether Hungarian or foreign. This is readily understandable, for these were the styles with which the company was most familiar. Their performances show less evidence of the influence of the more modern forms, of styles and genres (modern dancing, jazz dancing and the symphonic ballet).

Of course, we have to remember that any company is made up of a number of gifted individuals and the characteristics of a company are not quite those which apply when we consider the individual soloists and their art. There are a great many highly qualified soloists in the company and any account of the company as a whole must necessarily include sketches of some of these personalities.

That the style defines the dancers and the dancers define the style is not merely a paradox—at least not for the Budapest Ballet company. Naturally, the company contains all the basic types of dancers: classical, semi-character and character dancers, those who specialize in romantic or modern dancing, those whose gift is more lyrical or dramatic. This individual flavour depends on personal physique, intellect, temperament, inclination and training; and it is also affected by the kind of parts they are most frequently asked to perform.

The basic features which determine the general character of the company are discernible in the artistic personality of the leading soloists, in fact these features are the ones which most clearly characterize their own artistic make-up and their performances. Classical training, a delivery that is full of feeling

127

and a well-developed acting skill are at the same time evident in the interpretations of the company as a whole.

It could be said that each one of the leading soloists knows and, in fact, dances practically every one of the leading roles in the repertoire. Their performances differ not in quality but only in the interpretation, each one bringing out or emphasizing some particular aspect of the part. All this ensures a uniformly high standard and a wealth of interpretation. It also helps individual artists in their development when they are called upon to perform different types of leading parts, for a variety of artistic assignments do not merely make demands on their skill and talent, but also form and enrich it. The girl who dances Giselle and Juliet, the *pas de deux* in *Kerchief* and in *The Girl Danced into Life*, the feminine lead in Bartók's *Music* and Flavia in *Spartacus* must be capable of portraying a fairy, a Shakespearian heroine, a Hungarian gipsy girl of the last century, a typical modern city girl, an intelligent woman of our times and a revolutionary of times past. She must be able to work out her roles and express herself in the various idioms of the art of dance whether classical, lyrical or national, and in the style of international jazz, expressive modern dance and modern neo-classical dance. The demanding nature of such a task does not need to be enlarged upon.

Leading prima ballerinas in the company who are required to undertake an exceptionally wide range of parts are Zsuzsa Kun and Adél Orosz. Both of them are well known as outstanding exponents of both Hungarian dancing and that of other nations. Any consideration of their artistic personalities must begin with a reference to ways in which they resemble each other. They were both pupils of Nádasi and studied for some time in the Soviet Union, and both of them dance more or less the same parts; moreover, each of them has visited many different parts of the world, both with the company and as individual guest artists.

There are, however, marked differences between them, and this enables them to complement each other very well and balance the character of the company as a whole.

Zsuzsa Kun's renderings are poetic, subtle and highly sensitive, intellectually and emotionally fervent, with a style and technique of great clarity. The glowing quality of her art can perhaps be most fully appreciated in her highly individual renderings of Giselle and Juliet. Her Giselle suggests a being at once romantic and with a responsiveness that is truly modern, a frail, beautiful and suffering creature. Her vivid portrait of Juliet is a unique blend of poetry and drama. At home and abroad she is looked upon as a prima ballerina of the classical-dramatic school, but because of her portrayals of the more intellectual heroines of the *Sacre*, *The Miraculous Mandarin*, *Music* and *Spartacus* she deserves to be acknowledged as a worthy exponent of modern works too; moreover her repertoire is even more comprehensive than we have indicated here.

Zsuzsa Kun commenced her studies in 1943 in the ballet school attached to the Opera House and she danced her first part (as a result of which she was awarded a scholarship and was officially accepted as a member of the company) at the age of 15 in the ballet entitled *The Fairy Doll*. In 1950, after several solo assignments in *Nutcracker* and *The Flames of Paris*, she was given a longer contract, and in 1952 she was officially appointed to be a soloist. Her first lead (that same year) was Zarema in *The Fountain of Bakhchisarai*, and from then on she was given a leading part in every production of ballets already in the repertoire and also in new productions. Of these, the most important, apart from those already mentioned, have been Odette-Odile in *Swan Lake*, Aurora in *The Sleeping Beauty*, and the principal female parts in *Romeo and Juliet*, *Chopiniana*, *Sheherazade*, and *Firebird*. In 1953 she won the second prize in the ballet contest at the World Festival of Youth and Students in Bucharest, and at the same Festival competition in 1955, held in Warsaw, she was awarded a first prize. In 1960 she won the Liszt Prize, in 1962 the Kossuth Prize, the highest award offered by the state for artists in Hungary, and in 1968 she was named an Artist of Merit of the Hungarian People's Republic.*

Adél Orosz's style is characterized by an intimate informality, an airy lightness combined with forcefulness, the technique of a virtuoso and a gift for rendering in forms that are harmonious and intelligible. These attributes are especially evident in those parts in which the interpretation is determined by the unique beauty and richness of form associated with classical dancing. This is the case, for instance, in the leading female roles in *The Sleeping Beauty*, *Nutcracker* and *Swan Lake*; also Jeanne in *The Flames of Paris*, the Princess in *The Wooden Prince*, the title role in *Sheherazade*, and various pieces specially selected for the concert platform. Her feeling for style and her training serve her well not only in the classic roles but also in the neo-classical duets in *Daphnis and Chloe*; her playful humour is very evident in *Coppélia* and *Promenade Concert*, while her dramatic ability is most clearly seen in the Soviet ballet dramas and particularly in her rendering of Flavia in *Spartacus*.

She commenced her studies in 1947 at the ballet school of the Opera House, and then in 1950 she moved on to the State Ballet Institute. Four years later she received her diploma and was given a contract with the company at the Opera House. It was not long before she was being given solo parts and in 1957 at the Youth Festival in Moscow she came first in the ballet contest, after which she was promoted to the position of soloist at the Opera. In 1964 she was chosen for the principal part in the Hungarian dance film entitled *The Girl Danced into Life*, in which she gave uniformly excellent performances of Hungarian folk dancing, classical dancing and jazz dancing. For her artistic achievement she was awarded the Liszt Prize in 1961 and the Kossuth Prize in 1965.

We have stressed the classical training of these two ballerinas and their talent for dancing in this style; but in the case of Gabriella Lakatos we must emphasize that her individual qualities are closely linked with the character and style of the company as a whole. Her dancing is informed with elemental force and restrained passion, a joyous zest for life, and a gift for drama that allows her to portray a wide range of characters. She has been able to interpret all her parts in a highly individual way to suit her own personality; in fact most of these roles were actually written for her and when this was not the case she invariably devised a memorable interpretation characteristic of a particular phase in the development of the company. In Harangozó's choreography for *The Miraculous Mandarin* the role of the Streetwalker has become identified with the personality of Gabriella Lakatos, and it is she who has very largely helped to turn this production into one of the most universally celebrated productions of the Budapest Ballet company.

Other leading roles associated with the name of Gabriella Lakatos are the heroine of *Bolero*, Aysa in *Gayane*, Odile in *Swan Lake*, the Woman in the *Polovtsian Dances*, Zarema in *The Fountain of Bakhchisarai*, Jeanne in *The Flames of Paris*, Rose in *Mischievous Students*, the Primadonna in *Promenade Concert*, the title role of *Coppélia*, and the two principal female roles in *Don Quixote*.

Gabriella Lakatos was also a Nádasi pupil, and she, too, completed her studies in the Ballet School of

---

* In 1971 she was awarded the distinction of Outstanding Artist.

129

the Opera House. She played her first important star role in 1947 in *The Three-cornered Hat*. She accompanied the *corps de ballet* on their foreign tours and was also invited to give many individual guest performances in several European countries. In recognition of her work she received the Kossuth Prize in 1958, and the title Artist of Merit in 1966.*

Following several successful performances in a number of leading roles Klotild Ugray won a place for herself as one of the leading soloists in the company. Her sound knowledge of classical dancing, her polished style and her tasteful and restrained interpretation of parts are best seen in her rendering of Maria in *Nutcracker*, Myrthe in *Giselle*, and the Lilac Fairy in *The Sleeping Beauty*. This means that the so-called "white" parts, in which a high standard of technique heightens the pure beauty of the dancing, are most suited to her personality. But she was also praised as the Princess in *The Wooden Prince*, and in the title roles of *Firebird* and *Sheherazade*.

Klotild Ugray has been at the Opera as a member of the company since 1950, and she was promoted to be a soloist in 1952. She danced her first leading role in the *Nutcracker*. At the ballet contest of the World Festival of Youth and Students in Vienna she won a first prize. In 1964 she was awarded the Liszt Prize for her artistic achievement.

Jacqueline Menyhárt can also be listed as one of the company's leading soloists specializing in classical and lyrical dancing. Her interpretations are pleasingly poetic, her movements beautifully flowing and she has great sureness of style and technique. Some of her most outstanding performances have been as Maria in *The Fountain of Bakhchisarai*, also Juliet and Chloe, the Diamond in *The Sleeping Beauty*, and Flavia in *Spartacus*.

In 1964 she graduated from the State Ballet Institute where she had been in Nádasi's class and was given a contract in the same year to dance at the Opera. During the season of 1963–64 she had the opportunity of studying at the Bolshoi Theatre in Moscow. In 1968 she was awarded the Liszt Prize.

Vera Szumrák is another young dancer who received both her diploma and contract to the Opera in 1954. She is particularly well suited, by temperament and because of her classical training, for those leading roles which call for an intensity of passion and eroticism. Her mature style creates beautiful patterns of movement, her art is both dynamic and deeply expressive, and for this reason she gives significant performances as the Streetwalker in *The Miraculous Mandarin*, Zarema in *The Fountain of Bakhchisarai*, Aysa in *Gayane* and as Juliet, and Flavia in *Spartacus*. The classical and lyrical qualities of her dancing are fully realized in her rendering of the Lilac Fairy in *The Sleeping Beauty* and Myrthe in *Giselle*; this latter role gave her first lead in 1958.

Mária Kékesi** has developed a style that is pure, restrained and of an almost crystal-like clarity. Physically and intellectually she is best suited to the "white" parts. The two principal female roles in *Swan Lake*, the Mazurka in *Chopiniana*, Myrthe in *Giselle*, the Princess in *The Wooden Prince*, and the title role of *Firebird* have much in common, though it may be that it is Kékesi who brings them closer to each other. In each case her interpretation is built on a splendidly harmonious and precise exposition of classical dancing, in which she received a basic training at the State Ballet Institute. In 1959, when she graduated, she was immediately asked to join the company at the Opera. In 1964, at the International Ballet Competition in Varna she was awarded a bronze medal.

    * In 1971 she was awarded the distinction of Outstanding Artist.
    ** She was awarded the Liszt Prize in 1970.

130

One of the male soloists, Viktor Fülöp, has had a career as a dancer that spans the entire post-war period of Hungarian ballet, and he has greatly contributed to the development of ballet in this country. His fluid personality ensures that he is well suited to a variety of styles, but he is most successful in his portrayal of those heroes who can only be brought to life through the poetry and dynamism of dancing and the acting ability of the artist. This explains the unforgettable quality of his interpretation of the two great revolutionary heroes of Hungarian ballet—Philippe *(The Flames of Paris)* and Spartacus—and this is why he is so good as the majestic barbarian Ghirei Khan in *The Fountain of Bakhchisarai*, the passionate Young Moor in *Sheherazade*, Baltaváry, the Hungarian reformer of noble birth in *Bihari's Song* or the Mandarin, monumental and invincible. Indeed we might go through the whole list of ballets in the repertoire, for in most of them Viktor Fülöp has given great performances, as the romantic Prince in *Giselle*, for instance, as Francis in *Coppélia*, and in the role of folk hero in *Gayane* and the *Polovtsian Dances*.

Viktor Fülöp also began his studies under Nádasi, in 1937. He was given his first important solo part ten years later as the prince in *The Wooden Prince*, and in the next year he played the title role of *Petrouchka*. Between 1950 and 1960 he danced the leading male role in every single ballet that has been produced in Hungary, and during the nineteen-sixties he also gave excellent performances in a number of dance-dramas. In 1953 he received a prize at the Youth Festival, in 1960 he was awarded the Liszt Prize, two years later the Kossuth Prize, and in 1968 the title Artist of Merit was conferred on him.* He has made frequent tours abroad both with the company and as an individual guest artist; and he has several times stayed in Moscow for lengthy periods in order to study at the Bolshoi Theatre. For several years now he has been one of the company's ballet masters.

Viktor Róna is the leading classical soloist of the Budapest Ballet. He is the best known Hungarian ballet dancer in Hungary and he is seen abroad more frequently than any other artist in the company. Most significant are his classical performances in the *Nutcracker*, *Swan Lake*, *Giselle* and *The Sleeping Beauty*, and his renderings of the male title roles in *Romeo and Juliet* and in *Daphnis and Chloe* are outstanding.

At the same time Róna gives splendid performances in most character parts. He is outstanding as Philippe, Spartacus, Mercutio and Armen (the latter in *Gayane*); the varied nature of these performances gives ample evidence of the range of his acting, his ability to interpret character and his general versatility as an artist.

From 1945 to 1950 Viktor Róna studied at the Ballet School of the Opera House, continuing his training until 1954 at the State Ballet Institute where he was one of Nádasi's pupils. He was given his first leading role a year after his graduation, in the *Nutcracker*, and since 1957 he has been a soloist.

In 1955 at the World Festival of Youth and Students in Warsaw he was given a third prize in the ballet contests, and in 1959, in Vienna, he was awarded a first prize. Together with Adél Orosz, who is his constant partner, he studied for one year in Leningrad. In 1963 he was awarded the Liszt Prize and in 1965 the Kossuth Prize.

Ferenc Havas's dancing is deeply emotional and this is perhaps the most striking aspect of his art, although he is also a gifted actor and his technique is of a high order. He too has played almost every

* In 1971 he was awarded the distiction of Outstanding Artist.

leading role in the company's repertoire. His most notable performances are in *Coppélia*, *Romeo and Juliet*, *The Wooden Prince*, *The Fountain of Bakhchisarai*, *Sheherazade*, and *Gayane*.

He joined the children's corps at the Opera in 1947, in 1950 he won a scholarship, and two years later was given a contract with the company. He was a prize winner at the World Festival of Youth and Students in Bucharest in 1953 and was promoted to be a soloist in the same year. In 1964 he was given an award to enable him to study at the Bolshoi Theatre in Moscow. He took part in all the foreign tours made by the company and on a number of occasions he was also invited to visit other countries as a guest artist. For his successes at home and abroad he was awarded the Liszt Prize in 1963 and the Kossuth Prize in 1965.

The art of Levente Sipeki is characterized by an attractive youthful spontaneity and a dry humour, qualities which have made it inevitable that he should be given certain character parts; his dancing is also powerfully dramatic and he displays a sure touch in his interpretation of the classical style, though he is also a gifted actor. Accordingly his most significant parts have been: the Prince in the *Nutcracker* and *Giselle*, the male lead in the *pas de trois* in *Swan Lake* and the *Classical Symphony*, Vatslav in *The Fountain of Bakhchisarai*, the poet in *Chopiniana*, character parts in *The Sleeping Beauty* (Blue Bird), *Mattie the Gooseboy*, Eager-Beaver Joe in *Mischievous Students*, the title role of *Petrouchka*, Gad in *Spartacus*, and several performances for the concert platform. He danced the male lead in the dance film *The Girl Danced into Life*, made in 1964.

Levente Sipeki completed his studies at the State Ballet Institute in 1957. In the same year he won a first prize in the ballet contest of the World Festival of Youth and Students in Moscow, and was also given a contract to dance with the Budapest Ballet at the Opera House. Within a year he had been made a soloist. He has travelled and studied in the Soviet Union, and he often gives guest performances abroad in addition to his appearances with the company. He won the Liszt Prize in 1964.

Imre Dózsa is a classical dancer whose movements are particularly harmonius. His technique is excellent and his performances are outstanding for the purity of his style and the beautiful patterns created by his flowing movements. He received high praise for his performances in the *Nutcracker*, *Swan Lake*, *Giselle*, *The Sleeping Beauty*, *Romeo and Juliet*, *Daphnis and Cloe*, *The Firebird*, *The Fountain of Bakhchisarai*, *Music for Strings, Percussion and Celesta*, *Spartacus*, *The Wooden Prince* and *Coppélia*.

Imre Dózsa completed his studies at the State Ballet Institute in 1959, since when he has been a member of the company. In the same year that he graduated he was given a contract to join the company at the Opera and his first leading role was in *Bihari's Song*; then in 1964 he was promoted to be a soloist. Together with Mária Kékesi he was awarded a fellowship to study in Leningrad in 1967. The year before that he had won the Liszt Prize.

HARD WORK BEHIND THE SCENES

There are two kinds of ballet companies, those attached to a definite theatre or place, and those that tour the world. Members of the latter are drawn from all parts of the world; of course, foreign artists are also frequently offered contracts with companies permanently resident in one place.

One characteristic feature of the Budapest Ballet is that its members come to it from the State Ballet Institute which is situated almost next door to the Opera House; and as soon as they start their second year of training, when they are only eleven years old, the students from the Institute regularly perform in the company's productions, including the ballet inserts of the operas. Thus the students grow up in the atmosphere of the Opera, and quickly become accustomed to the discipline of the theatre with its written and unwritten rules. And when after graduation they join the *corps de ballet* and take their place among the adult dancers, they are still apprentices on trial. Later, they are admitted to the Third Quadrille from which, if they work hard and show talent, they can hope for gradual promotion from one quadrille to another. Some of them achieve the rank of titular soloist, but only a very few of them reach the coveted status of soloist. In this system star soloists will have been trained in just the same way, and in the same school, as their colleagues in the chorus, and they too will have had their share of the small parts. Ballet masters are also promoted from the ranks, that is, they have always danced in the chorus or have been soloists with the company. Members of the chorus, soloists and ballet masters all receive a special bonus after 25 years—and some receive another after 40 years—for loyal service to the theatre. They leave the Opera House only when the time comes for them to give up dancing. The company's leading artists are the paragons on whom a younger generation are expected to model themselves and who will in turn become models for yet another generation. It will be readily appreciated that this system has favoured the development within the Opera of a national company with a highly individual character of its own. The company resembles some living organism in that new members are quickly assimilated and the individual members, however different from each other, are united by the cohesive force of the collective spirit.

The dancers rehearse their own solo parts before joining the company for complete rehearsals. Their arrival on the stage is always something of a festive occasion, an interesting and exciting moment for the entire company. The artists sit in a great circle and even some of the office workers appear, keeping their fingers crossed for their favourites. The artists dancing solo parts are aware that they are performing before a most exacting forum of experts. If the performance is worthy of appreciation, the entire company bursts into applause. Then the soloists are given a genuine sense of assurance and feel that they can look forward with equanimity to the forthcoming première. But if an artist is not applauded, he or she has to overcome a feeling of fear and insecurity which lasts until the time of the first performance. Once he is facing the audience, however, the artist knows that everyone, every single member of the company, is ardently hoping for success. But if any dancer gives a poor performance and his efforts are received in silence, he knows that he will be called to account before the ballet master or even the director.

The company has a very definite character of its own, not easy to describe because of its complexity, while there are also certain aspects which change continually according to the particular artist most in the limelight at any one period.

The fact that individual parts can be so variously interpreted sometimes creates a tense atmosphere in the building and can also bring about very amusing situations. There is both drama and humour in the scenes that take place around the bench under the notice-board on the main landing of the staircase where details of programmes, times of rehearsals and other announcements are pinned up. This is the main "forum" of the company, a forum which is in no small measure responsible for ensuring that all the dramatic, lyrical and comic potentialities of every scene and dance are fully realized in every production.

In yet another sense there are two companies: the male and the female. For many years the profession was dominated by women who were usually more gifted artists than the men. There were few male dancers and, apart from one or two really outstanding soloists, the men were less knowledgeable, not so well trained, and certainly both less hard-working and talented than the women. As there were so many girls in the profession, it followed that there were many more girls than men with the ability to rise to the top of the profession, and therefore the competition to get parts was much greater among the girls than among the men who, as they were relatively few in number, were never short of desirable roles. Consequently the men could gain promotion and earn higher salaries more easily than the women. Among the soloists this situation had already changed by the end of the nineteen-forties, but in the chorus the improvement did not come about until much later. Only after the establishment of the State Ballet Institute did the situation become radically different. As the result of a nation-wide search for talent, begun in 1950 and continued for several years, and because of the growing popularity of ballet, more boys were coming forward with the wish to dance. The examination committee of the Ballet Institute made every effort over a period of years to recruit a suitable number of male dancers for the company. The young boys admitted to the school in the nineteen-fifties have since grown up, and today the company's male corps is as good as the female corps—not only in character parts, but in classical dancing too.

The Budapest Ballet performs in two theatres, the Hungarian State Opera House and the Erkel Theatre. The company gives an average of from ten to twelve full-length ballet programmes every month, some at the Opera House and some at the Erkel. In addition, the company also performs the ballet inserts in the operas, some of which are as long as a one-act ballet.

In Budapest there is an informed and enthusiastic audience for ballet, composed of men and women from many different sections of society. In the early days of the company, it was merely as a spectacle that ballet appealed to audiences, but present-day audiences respond to the beauties and react to the faults of the performances with professional sensitivity. The adults of today look back on V. I. Vainonen's interpretation of Tchaikovsky's *Nutcracker* as one of the most thrilling experiences of their childhood. The children of today can see *Swan Lake*, and the rest of the repertoire, in performances arranged specially for young people to give them the opportunity of learning to appreciate the art of ballet. Even today it is the young people who are the most responsive members of the ballet audiences. It is true that artists are inspired by any spontaneous outbreak of applause from an appreciative audience, but it is equally true to say that the dancers in the company find the special performances for young people more stimulating than any others.

In addition to their regular performances at home, members of the Budapest Ballet are often invited to perform abroad. They are unable to accept every invitation, their time for travel being limited by their responsibilities at home—rehearsals for new ballet inserts and new ballet productions as well as for the pieces regularly included in the repertoire.

Two of their numerous guest performances deserve special mention: one in Paris and one in Moscow. In Paris they attended the First International Dance Festival in 1963, and won the Gold Star Prize awarded to the best ensemble.* The members of the company will never forget the response of the Parisian audience: it was a revelation to them. It had the effect of making the company feel quite at home in the Théâtre des Champs-Élysées. Two years later, in 1965, the Hungarian dancers had a similar encounter with the Moscow public—just as independent, spoilt and fastidious as any audience in Paris. But *The Miraculous Mandarin*, *Swan Lake* (Act II), *The Flames of Paris* and *Chopiniana* were given a reception that can never be forgotten.

More recently, in 1968, the company found an unusually enthusiastic audience in the far north—at the Bergen Festival in Norway. After the final performance, the Festival director, Dr. M. Oftedal mounted the stage to take leave of the company before the applauding audience. Among other things he said: "With your high standard of ballet dancing you have conjured up for us a refreshing vision of spring, you have given us something we have never experienced before. Your performances have enchanted the Festival audiences and I hope that the warmth of their response will repudiate forever the myth that here in the frozen North we are so cold-blooded as to keep polar bears on the leash. We can also be wholeheartedly enthusiastic about anything worthy of that emotion, and now we have found something— your art. Never before have we expressed our thanks so wholeheartedly, and never before have we said with greater conviction: 'Au revoir!' "

It was not only the director of the Festival in Bergen who praised the company, for the following lines have been taken from French and Russian reviews: "They gave a spellbinding performance full of lyricism; they brought poetry to the stage... The audience listened with bated breath, hardly daring to applaud when the curtain rose, they were so enthralled by what they saw. But they certainly made up for this restraint when they clapped without ceasing at the end of the performance." (Antoine Goles, *Libération*, November 27, 1963) "Hungary today can be proud of her serious and distinctively national contribution to the art of classical ballet, which has been vividly demonstrated during the performances given by our guests now in Moscow." (Nicolai Elias, *Sovietskaya Kultura*, July 3, 1965)

Between such happy occasions as these when the company is praised and applauded at home or abroad, there are, of course, long intervals of hard work behind the scenes. Forever ambitious for improvement, never completely satisfied with themselves, members of the company attend daily sessions for exercise, practice or rehearsal. And at present their working conditions are not ideal: there are no facilities for training at the Erkel Theatre and though there are rehearsal rooms at the Opera House, the number of ballet rooms amount to "one and a half". So that they could put in the necessary hours of rehearsal,

---

* In 1969 the company won the prize again.

135

the dancers unanimously agreed to begin their daily routine earlier and to finish later than other members of the theatre. For this inspired company is immensely hard-working and ambitious. The company consists of only 106 artists and individual assignments are therefore heavy, demanding the maximum of everyone.* Conditions are expected to improve considerably, however, during the next few years. There has been more financial security for ballet dancers since 1967 when they became eligible for a retirement pension after 25 years of service; and the plan to increase the number of dancers in the company and to provide a new ballet room will ensure more favourable working conditions. But we must hope that these improvements will not encourage the dancers to pamper themselves or lose any of their present zeal for work.

There is a director who is ultimately responsible for the company, but he is advised by a staff of ballet masters.** The ballet masters work out among themselves a schedule of rehearsals, decide on the casting, help to interview and judge would-be entrants to the company when auditions are held and take part in discussions about promotions, pensions, salary increases and bonuses.

Each ballet master has his own peculiarly individual tasks: some of them are in charge of the practice periods and rehearsals, some direct rehearsals only, while others design choreographies as well as directing rehearsals.

The doyen of the ballet masters is Gyula Harangozó whose work as a choreographer and dancer we have already described. But Harangozó, the director of rehearsals has done as much to shape the company as Harangozó, the choreographer and dancer. At all rehearsals Gyula Harangozó has preferred to discard lengthy explanations in favour of a simple demonstration. And he was right, for a single movement by Harangozó is more eloquent than a stream of words. Nevertheless we must admit that it is not very easy to learn the steps by watching Harangozó's feet, for his movements are fast and concentrated, and though they seem effortless and natural, the rhythm is full of pitfalls. At any rate when Harangozó was directing rehearsals, the dancers certainly learned to "read feet". The ability to learn quickly is very important and the dancers are much appreciated for the speed with which they learn new parts.

Irén Hamala has been Harangozó's assistant and co-director at rehearsals since 1943. In 1950 she was promoted to be a soloist. And for nearly ten years now, Irén Hamala has been solely in charge of the daily rehearsals of the Harangozó pieces. It is owing to her remarkable memory that any Harangozó piece can be revived at any time. It was with her help that the company was able to revive *Promenade Concert* in 1968, although it had been taken out of the programme ten years earlier in 1958. Her method of rehearsals is analytical: she not only demonstrates the steps, but she breaks them down to their elements, and she defines every movement very precisely. Dynamic shading is also an important aspect in her method. As well as the Harangozó works she has also directed the rehearsals of works by other choreographers since 1943. Her repertoire consists of *Bolero, Queen of Sheba* (ballet insert), *The Fountain of Bakhchisarai, Music for Strings, Percussion and Celesta, Gayane Suite, Chopiniana, Petrouchka* and *Laurencia*.

---

* In 1971 the company consists of 112 artists.
** Since September, 1969, the staff of ballet masters functions as an Art Advisory Board as well. Its members are: Ágoston Balog, Éva Éhn, Viktor Fülöp, Gyula Harangozó, Zsuzsa Kun, Adél Orosz, Viktor Róna and László Seregi.

136

Viktor Fülöp is responsible for most of the great full-length classical and romantic works. In 1958 Lavrovsky entrusted him with the most important of the classical ballets, *Giselle*, asking him to keep an eye on the production, which initially he—Lavrovsky—had staged, and to maintain its pure style. Prior to this Viktor Fülöp had spent some time in the Soviet Union, studying at the Bolshoi Theatre in Moscow. There he absorbed the professional atmosphere of Russian ballet and adapted the Bolshoi style, the ideal style for classical ballet. In 1965 he returned to the Bolshoi Theatre for two more years of study. In his teaching of the classical dances Viktor Fülöp searches for the "melody" of movement, of the "cantilena" of feet, arms, upper body, head, and hands. He does not deal with static poses, but with the path described by the body before arriving at a given pose, and the path that leads to the next stage. In this conception space is primarily dynamic and not static. And time is the relationship between the path travelled and music.*

Margit Horváth is no longer an active member of the staff. She retired in 1967, but her work before that date during most of the period discussed here greatly contributed to the company's achievements. In 1950 she took charge of the two great ballets originally rehearsed with V. I. Vainonen: the *Nutcracker* and *The Flames of Paris*, and a year later she also took over *Swan Lake*. She was highly praised for her revival of *The Flames of Paris* (1959) which brought glory to the company when they performed it in Moscow in 1965. Her temperamental personality was given full scope when she rehearsed the character dances and the great crowd scenes in *The Flames of Paris*. In addition to supervising the great Russian and Soviet ballets she was also responsible for maintaining Ernő Vashegyi's choreographic designs for *Valpurgis Night*. But it is the younger generation, her pupils in the ballet school, who are most indebted to Margit Horváth, for she was their ballet master and rehearsed with them for many years.

After Margit Horváth's retirement, the soloist Ágoston Balogh took over the training of the children. He was extremely well qualified for this task and, utilizing the lessons learned by his predecessor, he organized ballet education for young people in the modern manner.

László Seregi rehearses only the productions in which his own choreographies are used. But he is increasingly engaged in rehearsal work because he is continually creating new works.** The task of rehearsing a company is rather like that of an art teacher or that of the conductor when he rehearses with an orchestra. There are as many different ways of performing the task as there are art masters and conductors. Of course, the aim is always the same: to achieve the best possible interpretation of the work, to teach this and rehearse it in as short a time as possible, with the minimum of effort achieving the maximum of success. Every master goes about this task in his own way, in the manner best suited to his own personality. László Seregi's style of teaching involves not only exceptionally accurate communication of the material (he is precise as regards music and movement) but also a stimulating use of the spoken word. His comments are sometimes dramatic, sometimes ironic, but always to the point, convincing and even compelling. His words can fire and chill at one and the same time; he uses words to encourage, inspire or "whip" his pupils into action. It is a language that the dancers understand. Seregi danced for years shoulder to shoulder with them, he knows them and they know him, and that is why they work for him with such devotion.

---

* Beside *Giselle, Swan Lake, Romeo and Juliet* and *The Flames of Paris* are included in Fülöp's repertoire.
** Since 1971 he has been rehearsing *La Fille Mal Gardée* too.

Sándor Barkóczy also rehearses mainly his own works. He also took charge, however, of the *Daphnis and Chloe* and the recruiting-dance insert for the opera *János Háry*. He graduated from the choreographers' training school in Moscow in 1956. It was as a talented young folk dancer that he first attracted attention and it was thus that he was helped to come to Budapest and later given a scholarship to study in the Soviet Union. He joined the Budapest Ballet in 1957, and since 1961 has worked as a ballet master. His rehearsals are noted for the atmosphere of dynamic enthusiasm which he generates.

Contact with foreign ballet masters has significantly influenced the development of the company. The Soviet masters, Vainonen, Lavrovsky and Gusev, have exerted the strongest influence—as personalities, quite apart from the impact of their own works—on our own ballet masters and the manner in which they so skilfully conduct rehearsals. Vainonen left a lasting mark on the Budapest Ballet because of his reorganization of the entire company and because he represented the first, and therefore the most powerful, impact of the Soviet style of dancing. In his *Giselle* Lavrovsky contributed his ambitious and magical interpretation of the old romantic school of ballet. Finally, Gusev performed the professional feat of transplanting the "perfect example", *The Sleeping Beauty*.

We cannot now analyse or describe the work of the quest ballet masters. Let us, however, mention Imre Eck, who is a frequent guest of the company, and who, when he is rehearsing his pieces, exercises a strong influence on the dancers, always putting the finishing touches to his choreographies with the creative co-operation of the performing artists, and allowing them plenty of scope for improvisation.

There are, in addition to the ballet masters who are responsible for rehearsals, others who are in charge of the practice classes.

After the death of Ferenc Nádasi, Éva Éhn and Éva Géczy, the ballet masters in charge of the practice classes, found themselves in a thankless and difficult position. It was a hard task to follow a gifted artist like Ferenc Nádasi. For some time the company felt discouraged and dissatisfied. But the new ballet masters had been in charge of some of the exercises even under Nádasi and gradually they were accepted by the dancers. Since the autumn of 1963, Olga Lepeshinskaya has returned periodically as a guest ballet master. She builds up her lessons with compulsive logic, making every exercise serve a definite educational purpose. She gives phenomenal demonstrations of each individual exercise, humming the music to go with it, occasionally showing, with the greatest bravado, even the most difficult leaps (for instance, the *double saut de basque!*), a feat which both fascinates and inspires her pupils. Éva Éhn was promoted to be a soloist in 1950. She has been conducting practice classes since 1955, and since 1960 she has also been teaching at the State Ballet Institute. With the passage of time her exercises have become increasingly inventive and purposeful, so that they now include all the raw material of classical ballet. For some time she has deliberately chosen to concentrate all her energies on the education and training of ballet dancers. After several years' experience as a teacher and having also worked under Lepeshinskaya and spent some time in 1968 studying in Moscow, she has now developed her talent to the full and is at the height of her powers.

Éva Géczy became a soloist in 1950, and has conducted practice classes since 1951. In 1963 she spent some time studying in Leningrad. She composes exercises that are light and dance-like.*

* In September, 1969, Éva Géczy was appointed ballet master in Bonn.

Members of the company start the day—every day—by going to "school", that is, the practice class. As one group finishes another begins. The members of the new group look fresh, while those coming out from the previous lesson look somewhat dishevelled. These lessons last until noon. The hours from 12 until 2 are set aside for rehearsals of the large groups. After two there are always extra rehearsals. And from 5:30 p.m. until 9:30 p.m. there is a succession of solo and group rehearsals. Meantime, at seven o'clock, the curtain goes up in both theatres and performances are given—possibly an opera with a ballet insert in each of the three acts, or even an entire evening of ballet. And there in the limelight the tiring work in which they have been absorbed for so many days and nights, at last comes to fruition. The Budapest Ballet has just emerged from an important period of development. Now it goes forward, we believe, to fulfill a great promise.

107, 108

109–111

112, 113

APPENDIX

Compiled by G. P. Dienes

BALLET REPERTOIRE BETWEEN 1936 AND 1971

The following list includes not only first perform-ances, but also revivals which are essentially different from previous versions, in respect of choreography, scenery or costume, even though produced by the same person. Re-studied parts and new casts are not included.

The list is arranged chronologically. Each entry comprises the date, the title of the ballet, the genre and the names of the

Librettist (Lib.)
Composer (Mus.)
Director (Dir.)
Choreographer (Chor.)
Stage designer (Déc.)
Designer of costumes (Cost.)
Conductor (Cond.)
Principal dancers (Pr.)

References are made to earlier or later versions performed at the State Opera House, Budapest.

In the 1936–1937 Season

December 6, 1936

Scene in the Csárda
Ballet in two scenes
Lib.: Viktor Lányi
Mus.: Jenő Hubay
Dir. and chor.: Gyula Harangozó
Déc. and cost.: Zoltán Fülöp
Cond.: Jenő Kenessey
Pr.: Bella Bordy, Ilona Vera, Károly Zsedényi and
   Gyula Harangozó

February 25, 1937

Lysistrata
Ballet in one act
Lib.: Gusztáv Oláh, after Aristophanes
Mus.: László Lajtha

Dir.: Gusztáv Oláh
Chor.: Rezső Brada
Déc. and cost.: Zoltán Fülöp
Cond: János Ferencsik
Pr.: Piroska Tutsek, Bella Bordy, Ilona Vera,
   Melinda Ottrubay and Gyula Harangozó

June 3, 1937

Jankó in Boots
Fairy play in three scenes
Lib.: Ervin Clementis
Mus.: Jenő Kenessey
Chor.: Gyula Harangozó
Déc. and cost.: Gusztáv Oláh and Zoltán Fülöp
Cond.: Jenő Kenessey
Pr.: Gyula Harangozó and Karola Szalay

In the 1937–1938 Season

January 20, 1938

Polovtsian Dances
Ballet in one act
Lib. and mus.: A. P. Borodin *(Prince Igor)*
Chor.: Gyula Harangozó
Déc.: Gusztáv Oláh
Cost.: Tivadar Márk
Cond.: I. Dobroven
Pr.: Karola Szalay, Ilona Vera and
   Gyula Harangozó
Later: Gyula Harangozó, 1961

April 9, 1938

Salade
Ballet chanté, in two acts
Lib.: A. Flament
Mus.: D. Milhaud
Chor.: Gyula Harangozó
Déc. and cost.: Gusztáv Oláh

Cond.: Vilmos Rubányi
Pr.: Karola Szalay and Gyula Harangozó
Later: Gyula Harangozó, 1945
       Gyula Harangozó, 1962

In the 1938–1939 Season

October 27, 1938
Maria Veronica
Musical mystery in two parts
Lib.: András Rékai, after Margit Bethlen
Mus.: Jenő Ádám
Dir.: András Rékai
Chor.: Gyula Harangozó
Déc.: Gusztáv Oláh
Cond.: Vilmos Rubányi
Pr.: Karola Szalay

December 6, 1938
Picnic in May at Pozsony
Ballet in one scene
Lib.: János Fóthy
Mus.: Lajos Rajter
Chor.: Gyula Harangozó
Déc.: Gusztáv Oláh
Cost.: Tivadar Márk
Cond.: Jenő Kenessey
Pr.: Bella Bordy and Gyula Harangozó

February 26, 1939
Pot-pourri from *Sybill*
Mus.: Viktor Jacobi
Chor.: Gyula Harangozó
Cond.: Vilmos Rubányi
Pr.: Melinda Ottrubay, Hedvig Hidas,
   Karola Szalay, Ilona Vera and Gyula Harangozó

April 19, 1939
Romeo and Juliet
Poème dansé in one act
Lib.: after Shakespeare
Mus.: P. I. Tchaikovsky
Chor.: Gyula Harangozó
Déc. and cost.: Gusztáv Oláh
Cond.: Jenő Kenessey

Pr.: Zoltán Sallay, Ilona Vera, László Csányi,
   and Károly Zsedényi

In the 1939–1940 Season

November 10, 1939
The Wooden Prince
Fairy play in one act
Lib.: Béla Balázs
Mus.: Béla Bartók
Chor.: Gyula Harangozó
Déc. and cost.: Gusztáv Oláh
Cond.: S. Failoni
Pr.: Gyula Harangozó, Ilona Vera
   and Károly Zsedényi
Earlier: Ottó Zöbisch, 1917
       J. Cieplinski, 1935
Later: Ernő Vashegyi, 1952
      Gyula Harangozó, 1958
      László Seregi, 1970

May 24, 1940
Legend of the Nile
Dance legend in three scenes
Lib.: Klára Tüdős, after Th. Gautier
Mus.: Jenő Takács
Chor.: Gyula Harangozó
Déc.: Zoltán Fülöp
Cost.: Tivadar Márk
Cond.: Jenő Kenessey
Pr.: Karola Szalay, Zoltán Sallay and
   Ferenc Kőszegi

In the 1940–1941 Season

May 22, 1941
La Jarre
Dance comedy in one act
Lib.: L. Pirandello
Mus.: A. Casella
Dir. and chor.: Gyula Harangozó
Déc.: Gusztáv Oláh
Cost.: Tivadar Márk
Cond.: Jenő Kenessey
Pr.: Gyula Harangozó, László Csányi
   and Bella Bordy

December 5, 1941

The Unlucky Suitor
Ballet
Lib.: L. Hofman and Gyula Harangozó
Mus.: W. A. Mozart *(Les Petits Riens)*
Dir. and chor.: Gyula Harangozó
Déc.: Zoltán Fülöp
Cost.: Tivadar Márk
Cond.: Jenő Kenessey
Pr.: Gyula Harangozó and Melinda Ottrubay

April 22, 1942

Liebesträume
Ballet
Lib.: Géza Hanvay
Mus.: F. Liszt *(Les Préludes* and *Liebesträume)*
Dir. and chor.: Gyula Harangozó
Déc.: Gusztáv Oláh
Cost.: Tivadar Márk
Cond.: Jenő Kenessey
Pr.: Bella Bordy, Melinda Ottrubay
   and Károly Zsedényi

June 5, 1942

Les Créatures de Prométhée
Poème dansé, in two scenes
Lib.: Aurél Milloss, after S. Vigano
Mus.: Beethoven
Chor.: Aurél Milloss
Déc. and cost.: Gusztáv Oláh
Cond.: János Ferencsik
Pr.: László Csányi, Ilona Vera and Zoltán Sallay
Earlier: M. Guerra, 1913

In the 1942–1943 Season

December 12, 1942

Dream Play
Poème romantique dansé
Mus.: R. Schumann *(Carnival)*
   orchestrated by Otto Berg
Chor.: Aurél Milloss
Déc. and cost.: Gusztáv Oláh
Cond.: Jenő Kenessey

Pr.: Kató Patócs and György Tatár
Earlier: Milloss *(Carnival)*, 1935

December 30, 1942

Sylvia
Ballet in one act
Lib.: Ferenc Nádasi, after Barbier and Mérante
Mus.: L. Delibes
Dir. and chor.: Ferenc Nádasi
Déc. and cost.: Gusztáv Oláh
Cond.: Jenő Kenessey
Pr.: Melinda Ottrubay
Earlier: M. Guerra, 1904, 1916
   Troyanovsky, 1935

In the 1943–1944 Season

October 23, 1943

Serenade
Dances
Mus.: W. A. Mozart
Chor.: J. Cieplinski
Déc. and cost.: Gusztáv Oláh
Cond.: Jenő Kenessey
Pr.: Melinda Ottrubay, Margit Pintér, György
   Tatár, Bella Bordy and Károly Zsedényi

Kaiserwalzer
Dances
Mus.: Johann Strauss
Chor.: J. Cieplinski
Cond.: Jenő Kenessey
Pr.: Bella Bordy, Kató Patócs, Károly Zsedényi,
   Zoltán Sallay, Etelka Kálmán, Éva Géczy and
   Margit Pintér

Bolero
Dance scene
Lib.: J. Cieplinski
Mus.: M. Ravel
Chor.: J. Cieplinski
Déc.: Zoltán Fülöp
Cost.: Tivadar Márk
Cond.: Jenő Kenessey
Pr.: Melinda Ottrubay, Zoltán Sallay,
   György Tatár and Etelka Kálmán

December 5, 1943

Students of Debrecen
Dance comedy
Lib.: Miklós Laurisin, after Mór Jókai
Mus.: Miklós Laurisin
Chor.: J. Cieplinski
Déc.: Zoltán Fülöp
Cost.: Tivadar Márk
Cond.: Vilmos Rubányi
Pr.: Melinda Ottrubay and Gyula Harangozó

June 20, 1944

Dorothy
Funny ballet in five scenes
Lib.: Dénes Tóth, after Mihály Csokonai Vitéz
Mus.: Dénes Tóth
Chor.: J. Cieplinski
Dir.: Gusztáv Oláh
Déc.: Zoltán Fülöp
Cost.: Tivadar Márk
Cond.: Jenő Kenessey
Pr.: Erika Mihály, Rezső Brada, Margit Pintér,
    Éva Géczy, Erzsi Horváth, Etelka Kálmán,
    Kató Patócs, Károly Zsedényi and Zoltán Sallay

In the 1944–1945 Season

May 15, 1945

Salade
Ballet chanté in two acts
Lib.: A. Flament
Mus.: D. Milhaud
Dir. and chor.: Gyula Harangozó
Déc. and cost.: Gusztáv Oláh
Cond.: János Ferencsik
Pr.: Gyula Harangozó and Melinda Ottrubay
Earlier: Gyula Harangozó, 1938
Later: Gyula Harangozó, 1962

In the 1945–1946 Season

September 26, 1945

The Birthday of the Infanta
Pantomime in three scenes
Lib.: Miklós Radnai, after O. Wilde
Mus.: Miklós Radnai

Chor.: J. Cieplinski and Ferenc Nádasi
Déc. and cost.: Gusztáv Oláh and Zoltán Fülöp
Cond.: Jenő Kenessey
Pr.: Janina Szarvas, Zoltán Sallay and István Rab
Earlier: Ottó Zöbisch, 1918
        J. Cieplinski, 1936

December 9, 1945

Love Spell
Andalusian gipsy scene in one act
Lib.: G. Martinez Sierra
Mus.: M. de Falla
Chor.: J. Cieplinski
Déc.: Gusztáv Oláh
Cost.: Tivadar Márk
Cond.: S. Failoni
Pr.: Kató Patócs, György Tatár and
    Ernő Vashegyi

The Miraculous Mandarin
Dance pantomime in one act
Lib.: Menyhért Lengyel
Mus.: Béla Bartók
Chor.: Gyula Harangozó
Déc. and cost.: Gusztáv Oláh
Cond.: János Ferencsik
Pr.: Ernő Vashegyi and Melinda Ottrubay
Later: Gyula Harangozó, 1956
      László Seregi, 1970

December 31, 1945

American Rhapsody
Ballet in one scene
Mus.: G. Gershwin *(Rhapsody in Blue)*
Chor.: György Tatár and Imre Sziver
Déc.: Zoltán Fülöp
Cost.: Tivadar Márk
Cond.: Pál Varga
Pr.: Kató Patócs and György Tatár

New Year's Eve in Budapest
Dance scene
Mus.: F. Liszt
Dir.: Gusztáv Oláh
Chor.: Gyula Harangozó
Déc.: Zoltán Fülöp
Cond.: ꞇ ő Kenessey

154

Pr.: Melinda Ottrubay, Vera Pásztor, Zoltán Sallay
and Ernő Vashegyi

April 13, 1946

Sakuntala
Poème dansé in two scenes
Mus.: Károly Goldmark
Dir.: Gusztáv Oláh
Chor.: J. Cieplinski
Déc. and cost.: Gusztáv Oláh
Cond.: Jenő Kenessey
Pr.: Melinda Ottrubay and György Tatár

In the 1946–1947 Season

April 25, 1947

Divertimento
Dance suite
Mus.: Sándor Jemnitz
Chor.: J. Cieplinski
Déc.: Gusztáv Oláh
Cost.: Tivadar Márk
Cond.: Jenő Kenessey
Pr.: Dóra Csinády, István Sallay, Vera Pásztor,
Gyula Suba, Etelka Kálmán, László Tóth,
Viktor Fülöp, Gabriella Lakatos
and Ernő Vashegyi

The Three-cornered Hat
Ballet in one act
Lib.: G. Martinez Sierra
Mus.: M. de Falla
Chor.: Gyula Harangozó
Déc. and cost.: Gusztáv Oláh
Cond.: Jenő Kenessey
Pr.: Gabriella Lakatos, Zoltán Sallay and
Gyula Harangozó
Earlier: A. Gaubier, 1928
Later: Gyula Harangozó, 1959

In the 1947–1948 Season

February 27, 1948

Le Spectre de la Rose
Choreographic tableau
Lib.: L. I. Vaudoyer, after Th. Gautier

Mus.: C. M. von Weber, orchestrated by H. Berlioz
Chor.: Ferenc Nádasi
Déc.: Gusztáv Oláh
Cost.: Tivadar Márk
Cond.: Pál Varga
Pr.: Vera Pásztor and István Rab
Earlier: Ottó Zöbisch, 1919

L'Après-midi d'un Faune
Choreographic tableau
Mus.: C. Debussy
Chor.: J. Cieplinski
Déc.: Gusztáv Oláh
Cond.: Jenő Kenessey
Pr.: Ernő Vashegyi and Alice Erdélyi

Ancient Castle
Dance legend
Lib.: Béla Balázs
Mus.: Béla Bartók *(Dance Suite)*
Chor.: Gyula Harangozó
Déc. and cost.: Gyula Harangozó
Cond.: Jenő Kenessey
Pr.: Dóra Csinády and Zoltán Sallay

Promenade Concert
Ballet in one act
Lib.: Gyula Harangozó
Mus.: Johann Strauss, arranged by Jenő Kenessey
Dir. and chor.: Gyula Harangozó
Déc.: Zoltán Fülöp
Cost.: Tivadar Márk
Cond.: Jenő Kenessey
Pr.: Vera Pásztor, Zoltán Sallay, Gabriella Lakatos,
Gyula Harangozó and Ernő Vashegyi
Later: Gyula Harangozó, 1968

March 22, 1948

Introduction et Allegro
Mus.: M. Ravel
Chor.: J. Charrat
Déc. and cost.: Gusztáv Oláh

Concerto
Mus.: S. Prokofiev
Chor.: J. Charrat
Déc. and cost.: Gusztáv Oláh

Ballad
Mus.: F. Chopin
Chor.: J. Charrat
Déc. and cost.: Gusztáv Oláh

Red Shoe
Mus.: P.-G. Chaumette
Chor.: S. Lifar

Gipsy Melodies
Mus.: P. de Sarasate
Chor.: J. Charrat

Jeu de Cartes
Ballet in one act
Lib.: I. F. Stravinsky and Malaev
Mus.: I. F. Stravinsky
Chor.: J. Charrat
Déc. and cost.: Gusztáv Oláh

For the whole evening:
Cond.: Jenő Kenessey
Pr.: J. Charrat

In the 1948–1949 Season

November 27, 1948
Picnic in May at Pozsony
Ballet in one scene
Lib.: János Fóthy
Mus.: Jenő Kenessey
Dir. and chor.: Gyula Harangozó
Déc.: Gusztáv Oláh
Cost.: Tivadar Márk
Cond.: Jenő Kenessey
Pr.: Bella Bordy, Zoltán Sallay and
  Gyula Harangozó

June 19, 1949
Petrouchka
Ballet in four scenes
Lib.: A. Benois
Mus.: I. F. Stravinsky
Dir.: Gusztáv Oláh
Chor.: Ernő Vashegyi
Déc.: Gusztáv Oláh and Zoltán Fülöp
Cost.: Tivadar Márk

156

Cond.: András Kórodi
Pr.: István Rab, Vera Pásztor and Ernő Vashegyi
Earlier: Ede Brada, 1926
       Aurél Milloss, 1933
Later: M. Fokine, 1966

Mischievous Students
Ballet in six scenes
Lib.: Gusztáv Oláh, after Mór Jókai
Mus.: Ferenc Farkas
Dir. and chor.: Gyula Harangozó
Déc.: Zoltán Fülöp
Cost.: Tivadar Márk
Cond.: Jenő Kenessey
Pr.: Dóra Csinády, István Rab and
  Gyula Harangozó

In the 1949–1950 Season

February 19, 1950
Nutcracker
Ballet in three acts
Lib.: V. I. Vainonen, after E. T. A. Hoffmann
Mus.: P. I. Tchaikovsky
Chor.: V. I. Vainonen
Déc. and cost.: Gusztáv Oláh
Cond.: Jenő Kenessey
Pr.: Dóra Csinády, Viktor Fülöp
  and Gyula Harangozó
Earlier: Ede Brada, 1927

June 11, 1950
The Flames of Paris
Ballet in four acts
Lib.: N. D. Volkov and V. V. Dimitriev
Mus.: B. V. Asafiev
Dir. and chor.: V. I. Vainonen
Déc.: Zoltán Fülöp
Cost.: Tivadar Márk
Cond.: Jenő Kenessey
Pr.: István Rab, Nóra Kováts, Irén Hamala,
  Dóra Csinády, Ernő Vashegyi and János Ősi

In the 1950–1951 Season

March 8, 1951
Kerchief
Ballet in three acts

Lib.: Viktor Lányi, Gusztáv Oláh and
  Gyula Harangozó
Mus.: Jenő Kenessey
Dir. and chor.: Gyula Harangozó
Déc.: Zoltán Fülöp
Cost.: Tivadar Márk
Cond.: Jenő Kenessey
Pr.: Gabriella Lakatos, Viktor Fülöp,
  Nóra Kováts and István Rab

June 24, 1951
Swan Lake
Ballet in four acts
Lib.: V. P. Begichev and V. F. Geltser
Mus.: P. I. Tchaikovsky
Dir. and chor.: A. M. Messerer
Déc.: Gusztáv Oláh and Zoltán Fülöp
Cost.: Tivadar Márk
Cond.: Jenő Kenessey
Pr.: Nóra Kováts, István Rab and Ernő Vashegyi
Later: A. M. Messerer, 1969

In the 1951–1952 Season

March 15, 1952
The Wooden Prince
Ballet in one act
Lib.: Béla Balázs
Mus.: Béla Bartók
Chor.: Ernő Vashegyi
Déc. and cost.: Gusztáv Oláh
Cond:. János Ferencsik
Pr.: Viktor Fülöp, Nóra Kováts and István Rab
Earlier: Ottó Zöbisch, 1917
        J. Cieplinski, 1935
        Gyula Harangozó, 1939
Later: Gyula Harangozó, 1958
       László Seregi, 1970

April 29, 1952
The Fountain of Bakhchisarai
Ballet in four acts
Lib.: N. D. Volkov, after A. Pushkin
Mus.: B. V. Asafiev
Dir. and chor.: R. V. Zakharov
Déc.: Zoltán Fülöp

Cost.: Tivadar Márk
Cond.: Jenő Kenessey
Pr.: Vera Pásztor, Nóra Kováts, Viktor Fülöp,
  János Ősi and István Rab

In the 1952–1953 Season

April 24, 1953
Coppélia
Ballet in three acts
Lib.: Nuitter and Saint-Léon's book after
  E. T. A. Hoffmann, adapted by Gyula
  Harangozó
Mus.: L. Delibes, rearranged by Jenő Kenessey
Chor.: Gyula Harangozó
Déc.: Zoltán Fülöp
Cost.: Tivadar Márk
Cond.: Jenő Kenessey
Pr.: Nóra Kováts, Gyula Harangozó and István Rab
Earlier: M. Guerra, 1912
        J. Cieplinski, 1932

In the 1953–1954 Season
(No new ballets presented)

In the 1954–1955 Season

December 2, 1954
Bihari's Song
Ballet in four acts
Lib.: Lajos Bálint and Gusztáv Oláh
Mus.: Jenő Kenessey
Chor.: Ernő Vashegyi
Déc.: Zoltán Fülöp and Gusztáv Oláh
Cost.: Tivadar Márk
Cond.: Jenő Kenessey
Pr.: Vera Pásztor, Viktor Fülöp, Dóra Csinády
  and János Ősi

In the 1955–1956 Season

June 1, 1956
The Miraculous Mandarin
Dance pantomime in one act
Lib.: Menyhért Lengyel
Mus.: Béla Bartók
Dir. and chor.: Gyula Harangozó

Déc.: Zoltán Fülöp
Cost.: Tivadar Márk
Cond.: Jenő Kenessey
Pr.: Gabriella Lakatos and Ernő Vashegyi
Earlier: Gyula Harangozó, 1945
Later: László Seregi, 1970

In the 1956–1957 Season
(No new ballets presented)

In the 1957–1958 Season

February 16, 1958
Giselle
Ballet in two acts
Lib.: Th. Gautier
Mus.: A. Adam
Chor.: L. M. Lavrovsky, after J. Perrot,
  J. Coralli and M. Petipa
Déc.: Zoltán Fülöp
Cost.: Tivadar Márk
Cond.: Gedeon Fráter
Pr.: Zsuzsa Kun, Viktor Fülöp, Klotild Ugray,
  Adél Orosz and Viktor Róna

June 18, 1958
The Wooden Prince
Ballet in one act
Lib.: Béla Balázs
Mus.: Béla Bartók
Chor.: Gyula Harangozó
Déc.: Zoltán Fülöp
Cost.: Tivadar Márk
Cond.: Jenő Kenessey
Pr.: Klotild Ugray, Ferenc Havas and
  Ágoston Balogh
Earlier: Ottó Zöbisch, 1917
    J. Cieplinski, 1935
    Gyula Harangozó, 1939
    Ernő Vashegyi, 1952
Later: László Seregi, 1970

In the 1958–1959 Season

March 10, 1959
Gayane
Ballet in four acts

Lib.: N. A. Anisimova, after K. Derzhavin
Mus.: A. I. Khachaturian
Dir. and chor.: N. A. Anisimova
Déc.: Gábor Forray
Cost.: Gizella Szeitz
Cond.: Péter Tóth
Pr.: Zsuzsa Kun, Viktor Fülöp, Adél Orosz,
  Levente Sipeki, Gabriella Lakatos and
  Viktor Róna

June 5, 1959
Csongor and Tünde
Fairy ballet in six scenes
Lib.: Tamás Blum, András Mikó and Imre Eck,
  after Mihály Vörösmarty
Mus.: Leó Weiner
Chor.: Imre Eck
Déc.: Gábor Forray
Cost.: Tivadar Márk
Cond.: Tamás Blum
Pr.: Zsuzsa Kun, Viktor Fülöp and Gabriella
  Lakatos
Earlier: J. Cieplinski, 1930

In the 1959–1960 Season

December 17, 1959
The Three-cornered Hat
Ballet in one act
Lib.: G. Martinez Sierra
Mus.: M. de Falla
Dir. and chor.: Gyula Harangozó
Déc.: Zoltán Fülöp
Cost.: Tivadar Márk
Cond.: Péter Tóth
Pr.: Gabriella Lakatos, Ferenc Havas and
  Gyula Harangozó
Earlier: A. Gaubier, 1928
    Gyula Harangozó, 1947

Sheherazade
Ballet in one act and four scenes
Lib.: Gyula Harangozó, after A. Benois
Mus.: N. A. Rimsky-Korsakov
Dir. and chor.: Gyula Harangozó
Déc.: Gábor Forray
Cost.: Gizella Szeitz

Cond.: Jenő Kenessey
Pr.: Zsuzsa Kun, Viktor Fülöp, Zoltán Sallay and
Imre Eck
Earlier: R. Kölling, 1930

May 12, 1960
Mattie the Gooseboy
Ballet in three acts, seven scenes
Lib.: Gyula Harangozó, after Mihály Fazekas
Mus.: Ferenc Szabó
Dir. and chor.: Gyula Harangozó
Déc.: Zoltán Fülöp
Cost.: Tivadar Márk
Cond.: András Kórodi
Pr.: Levente Sipeki, Adél Orosz and
Gyula Harangozó

In the 1960–1961 Season

January 26, 1961
Polovtsian Dances
Ballet in one act
Lib. and Mus.: A. P. Borodin *(Prince Igor)*
Chor.: Gyula Harangozó
Déc.: Zoltán Fülöp
Cost.: Tivadar Márk
Cond.: Vilmos Komor
Pr.: Gabriella Lakatos, Zsuzsa Kun and
Ferenc Havas
Earlier: Gyula Harangozó, 1938

In the 1961–1962 Season

March 11, 1962

Salade
Ballet chanté in two acts
Lib.: A. Flament
Mus.: D. Milhaud
Chor.: Gyula Harangozó
Déc. and cost.: Gusztáv Oláh
Cond.: Gyula Borbély
Pr.: Gabriella Lakatos, Ferenc Havas, Klotild
Ugray and Levente Sipeki
Earlier: Gyula Harangozó, 1938
Gyula Harangozó, 1945

April 28, 1962
Romeo and Juliet
Ballet in three acts
Lib.: L. M. Lavrovsky, S. S. Prokofiev and
S. Radlov, after Shakespeare
Mus.: S. S. Prokofiev
Dir. and chor.: L. M. Lavrovsky
Déc. and cost.: M. Petrovsky, after P. Viliams
Cond.: János Ferencsik
Pr.: Zsuzsa Kun, Ferenc Havas, Viktor Róna,
Viktor Fülöp, Levente Sipeki and Klotild Ugray

In the 1962–1963 Season

March 31, 1963
Maiden of the Sea
Ballet in one act
Lib.: György Lőrinc
Mus.: Rezső Sugár
Dir. and chor.: György Lőrinc
Déc.: Gábor Forray
Cost.: Gizella Szeitz
Cond.: Péter Tóth
Pr.: Adél Orosz and Viktor Róna

Le Sacre du Printemps
Ballet in one act
Lib.: Imre Eck
Mus.: I. F. Stravinsky
Chor.: Imre Eck
Déc.: Zoltán Fülöp
Cost.: Tivadar Márk
Cond.: András Kórodi
Pr.: Zsuzsa Kun

In the 1963–1964 Season

May 9, 1964
Mario and the Magician
Ballet in one act
Lib.: András Pernye and István Láng,
after Th. Mann
Mus.: István Láng
Dir.: Viktor Fülöp
Chor.: Viktor Fülöp and Zsuzsa Kun
Déc.: Péter Makai
Cost.: Tivadar Márk

Cond.: Gyula Borbély
Pr.: Levente Sipeki, Viktor Fülöp,
    Adél Orosz, Zoltán Sallay and Zsuzsa Kun

In the 1964–1965 Season

April 6, 1965

Chopiniana (Les Sylphides)
Ballet in one act
Mus.: F. Chopin
Chor.: M. Fokine
Déc.: Gábor Forray
Cost.: Gizella Szeitz
Cond.: Gedeon Fráter and Tamás Hraskó
Pr.: Zsuzsa Kun, Klotild Ugray, Mária Kékesi
    and Viktor Róna

Interplay
Ballet in one act
Mus.: M. Gould
Chor.: N. Thomson
Déc. and cost.: Péter Makai
Cond.: Tamás Hraskó
Pr.: Edit Dévényi and Levente Sipeki

Miners' Ballad
Ballet in one act
Lib.: Imre Eck
Mus.: Rudolf Maros
Chor.: Imre Eck
Déc.: Zoltán Fülöp
Cost.: Tivadar Márk
Cond.: Péter Tóth
Pr.: Jacqueline Menyhárt

Music for Strings, Percussion and Celesta
Ballet in one act
Lib.: Imre Eck
Mus.: Béla Bartók
Chor.: Imre Eck
Déc.: Zoltán Fülöp
Cost.: Tivadar Márk
Cond.: Péter Tóth
Pr.: Zsuzsa Kun and Imre Dózsa

In the 1965–1966 Season

June 1, 1966
Daphnis and Chloe
Ballet in three parts
Lib.: M. Fokine, after Longos
Mus.: M. Ravel
Chor.: Imre Eck
Déc.: Zoltán Fülöp
Cost.: Tivadar Márk
Cond.: Péter Tóth
Pr.: Viktor Róna, Adél Orosz, Vera Szumrák
    and Imre Dózsa

Petrouchka
Ballet in four parts
Lib.: A. Benois and S. Boyarsky
Mus.: I. F. Stravinsky
Chor.: M. Fokine
Déc.: Gábor Forray
Cost.: Gizella Szeitz
Cond.: Gyula Borbély
Pr.: Levente Sipeki, Gabriella Lakatos and
    László Péter
Earlier: Ede Brada, 1926
        Aurél Milloss, 1933
        Ernő Vashegyi, 1949

Firebird
Ballet in two scenes
Lib.: M. Fokine
Mus.: I. F. Stravinsky
Chor.: M. Fokine
Déc.: Zoltán Fülöp
Cost.: Tivadar Márk
Cond.: Péter Tóth
Pr.: Zsuzsa Kun, Ferenc Havas and
    Jacqueline Menyhárt

In the 1966–1967 Season

September 27, 1966
Classical Symphony
Ballet in four movements
Mus.: S. S. Prokofiev
Chor.: Sándor Barkóczy
Déc.: Gábor Forray
Cost.: Gizella Szeitz

160

Cond.: Ervin Lukács
Pr.: Zsuzsa Kun, Levente Sipeki, Edit Dévényi
and József Forgách

May 14, 1967

The Sleeping Beauty
Ballet in three acts
Lib.: I. A. Vsevolozhsky and M. Petipa,
after Ch. Perrault
Mus.: P. I. Tchaikovsky
Chor.: P. Gusev, after M. Petipa
Déc.: Zoltán Fülöp
Cost.: Tivadar Márk
Cond.: Gedeon Fráter and Tamás Pál
Pr.: Zsuzsa Kun, Ferenc Havas, Klotild Ugray,
Tamás Koren, Edit Dévényi, Levente Sipeki
and Jacqueline Menyhárt

In the 1967–1968 Season

January 4, 1968

Promenade Concert
Ballet in one act
Lib.: Gyula Harangozó
Mus.: Johann Strauss, arranged by Jenő Kenessey
Dir. and chor.: Gyula Harangozó
Déc.: Gábor Forray
Cost.: Tivadar Márk
Cond.: Tamás Pál
Pr.: Adél Orosz, Levente Sipeki,
Gabriella Lakatos and Ferenc Havas
Earlier: Gyula Harangozó, 1948

Dance Suite
Symphonic ballet in six movements
Mus.: Béla Bartók
Chor.: Sándor Barkóczy
Déc.: Lajos Dömös
Cost.: Tivadar Márk
Cond.: Tamás Pál
Pr.: Adél Orosz, Viktor Róna and Imre Dózsa

Gayane Suite
Mus.: A. I. Khachaturian
Chor.: Viktor Fülöp, after N. A. Anisimova

Déc.: Gábor Forray
Cost.: Gizella Szeitz
Cond.: György Lendvai
Pr.: Zsuzsa Kun, Ferenc Havas, Gabriella Lakatos,
László Péter, Edit Dévényi and Levente Sipeki

May 18 and June 15, 1968

Spartacus
Ballet in three acts
Lib.: László Seregi
Mus.: A. I. Khachaturian
Dir. and chor.: László Seregi
Déc.: Gábor Forray
Cost.: Tivadar Márk
Cond.: Tamás Pál
Pr.: Viktor Fülöp, Zsuzsa Kun, Ferenc Havas,
Levente Sipeki, Zoltán Nagy, László Sterbinszky,
Vera Szumrák and Jacqueline Menyhárt, or Vik-
tor Róna, Adél Orosz, Imre Dózsa, László Ster-
binszky, Zoltán Fülöp, György Geszler, Katalin
Sebestyén and Mária Kékesi

In the 1968–1969 Season

April 6 and 7, 1969

Undine
Ballet in three acts
Lib.: Fr. Ashton, after F. H. K. de la Motte-Fouqué
Mus.: H. W. Henze
Dir. and chor.: Imre Eck
Déc.: Péter Makai
Cost.: Judit Gombár
Cond.: Tamás Pál and Gedeon Fráter
Pr.: Adél Orosz, Viktor Fülöp, Vera Szumrák
and Viktor Róna, or Mária Aradi, Ferenc Havas,
Mária Kékesi and Imre Dózsa

June 1 and 4, 1969

Swan Lake
Ballet in three acts
Lib.: V. P. Begichev and V. F. Geltser
Mus.: P. I. Tchaikovsky
Dir. and chor.: A. M. Messerer
Déc.: Lajos Dömös
Cost.: Gizella Szeitz

Cond.: Gedeon Fráter and Tamás Pál
Pr.: Zsuzsa Kun, Imre Dózsa and Tamás Koren,
   or Gabriella Lakatos, Ferenc Havas and László
   Pethő
Earlier: A. M. Messerer, 1951

In the 1969–1970 Season

March 22 and 25, 1970

Laurencia
Ballet in three acts
Lib.: Y. Mandelberg, after Lope de Vega
Mus.: A. Krein
Dir. and chor.: V. Chabukiani
Déc.: Gábor Forray
Cost.: Tivadar Márk
Cond.: Gedeon Fráter and Tamás Pál
Pr.: Adél Orosz, Viktor Róna, Mária Aradi and
   Jacqueline Menyhárt, or Mária Kékesi, Ferenc
   Havas, Ildikó Kaszás and Lilla Pártay

In the 1970–1971 Season

September 26 and 27, 1970

The Wooden Prince
Ballet in one act
Lib.: Béla Balázs
Mus.: Béla Bartók
Dir. and chor.: László Seregi
Déc.: Gábor Forray
Cost.: Tivadar Márk
Cond.: András Kórodi and Miklós Erdélyi
Pr.: Viktor Róna, Adél Orosz, Mária Kékesi and

József Forgách, or Imre Dózsa, Mária Kékesi,
   Katalin Csarnóy and Sándor Németh
Earlier: Ottó Zöbisch, 1917
   J. Cieplinski, 1935
   Gyula Harangozó, 1939
   Ernő Vashegyi, 1952
   Gyula Harangozó, 1958

The Miraculous Mandarin
Dance pantomime in one act
Lib.: Menyhért Lengyel
Mus.: Béla Bartók
Dir. and chor.: László Seregi
Déc.: Gábor Forray
Cost.: Tivadar Márk
Cond.: Miklós Erdélyi and András Kórodi
Pr.: Vera Szumrák and Viktor Fülöp, or Lilla Pár-
   tay and Ferenc Havas
Earlier: Gyula Harangozó, 1945
   Gyula Harangozó, 1956

March 28 and 30, 1971

La Fille Mal Gardée
Ballet in two acts
Lib.: Fr. Ashton, after J. Dauberval
Mus.: F. Hérold, adapted and arranged by
   J. Lanchbery
Dir. and chor.: Fr. Ashton
Déc.: Gábor Forray
Cost.: Tivadar Márk
Cond.: Gedeon Fráter and Tamás Pál
Pr.: Viktor Fülöp, Zsuzs Kun, Viktor Róna and
   Levente Sipeki; or László Pethő, Adél Orosz,
   Imre Dózsa and József Forgách

GUEST PERFORMANCES ABROAD BETWEEN 1936 AND 1971

Bayreuth

1936, October 20
Liszt: *Carnival in Budapest* (Ede Brada)
Liszt: *Hungarian Dreams* (J. Cieplinski)

Florence

1938, May 5
Liszt: *Carnival in Budapest*
Liszt: *Hungarian Dreams*

1938, May 7
Dohnányi: *Pierrette's Veil* (Elza Galafrés)
Hubay: *Scene in the Csárda*

1938, May 8
Liszt: *Hungarian Dreams*
Hubay: *Scene in the Csárda*

Bucharest (World Youth Festival)

1953, August 3
Kenessey: *Kerchief*

1953, August 4
Johann Strauss: *Promenade Concert*
Kenessey: *Kerchief*, Second act
Borodin: *Polovtsian Dances*

1953, August 5
Kenessey: *Kerchief*, Red Wine Csárdás, Third act

1953, August 6
Kenessey: *Kerchief*

1953, August 8
J. Strauss: *Promenade Concert*
Kenessey: *Kerchief*, Second act
Borodin: *Polovtsian Dances*

1953, August 9
Kenessey: *Kerchief*, Red Wine Csárdás, Third act

1953, August 10, 11
Delibes: *Coppélia*

Prague

1957, October 15, 16
Bartók: *The Miraculous Mandarin*
Kenessey: *Kerchief*
Johann Strauss: *Promenade Concert*

1957, October 18, 19
Delibes: *Coppélia*

Brno

1957, October 22
Bartók: *The Miraculous Mandarin*
Kenessey: *Kerchief*
Johann Strauss: *Promenade Concert*

1957, October 24
Delibes: *Coppélia*

Bratislava

1957, October 26
Delibes: *Coppélia*

1957, October 28
Bartók: *The Miraculous Mandarin*

Bucharest

1959, September 6, 7, 10
Bartók: *The Wooden Prince*
Farkas: *Mischievous Students*
Bartók: *The Miraculous Mandarin*

1959, September 8, 9
Adam: *Giselle*

Warsaw

1960, December 9, 10, 11 matinée and evening
Bartók: *The Wooden Prince*
Kenessey: *Kerchief*
Bartók: *The Miraculous Mandarin*

Poznań

1960, December 14, 15 matinée and evening
Concert programme
Kenessey: *Kerchief*, Second act
Bartók: *The Miraculous Mandarin*

Wrocław

1960, December 18, 19, 20
Concert programme
Kenessey: *Kerchief*, Second act
Bartók: *The Miraculous Mandarin*

Turin

1961, September
Bartók: *The Miraculous Mandarin*

Berlin

1961, October 14
Bartók: *The Wooden Prince*
Bartók: *The Miraculous Mandarin*
Farkas: *Mischievous Students*

1961, October 15
Adam: *Giselle*

Dresden

1961, October 17
Concert programme
Bartók: *The Miraculous Mandarin*
Farkas: *Mischievous Students*

Helsinki

1962, May 24, 25
Adam: *Giselle*, Second act
Bartók: *The Miraculous Mandarin*
Farkas: *Mischievous Students*

1962, May 26, 27, 28
Concert programme

1962, May 29, 30, 31
Khachaturian: *Gayane*

Edinburgh

1963, August 19, 20, 21, 23
Bartók: *The Wooden Prince*
Bartók: *The Miraculous Mandarin*

1963, August 22, 24
Farkas: *Mischievous Students*
Concert programme
Khachaturian: *Gayane*, Third act

Paris

1963, November 20, 21, 22, 23
Bartók: *The Wooden Prince*
Concert programme
Bartók: *The Miraculous Mandarin*

Helsinki

1964, June 1, 2, 3
Tchaikovsky: *Swan Lake*, Second act
Concert programme
Borodin: *Polovtsian Dances*

Stockholm

1964, June 5, 6, 7
Bartók: *The Wooden Prince*
Concert programme
Bartók: *The Miraculous Mandarin*

Cairo

1964, December 9, 10, 13
Bartók: *The Wooden Prince*
Tchaikovsky: *Swan Lake*, Second act
Bartók: *The Miraculous Mandarin*

1964, December 11, 12
Adam: *Giselle*, Second act
Concert programme
Khachaturian: *Gayane*, Kurdish Scene

1964, December 13, matinée
Tchaikovsky: *Swan Lake*, Second act
Concert programme
Khachaturian: *Gayane*, Kurdish Scene

Moscow

1965, June 25, 26, 27, July 4
Bartók: *The Wooden Prince*
Chopiniana
Bartók: *The Miraculous Mandarin*

1965, June 29, July 1
Maros: *Miners' Ballad*

Tchaikovsky: *Swan Lake*, Second act
Farkas: *Mischievous Students*

1965, July 2, 3
Asafiev: *The Flames of Paris*

Monte Carlo

1965, December 24, 25, 26
Chopiniana
Bartók: *The Miraculous Mandarin*
Borodin: *Polovtsian Dances*

1965, December 28, 29
Bartók: *Music for Strings, Percussion and Celesta*
Concert programme
Asafiev: *The Fountain of Bakhchisarai*, Selection

1965, December 31,
1966, January 1, 2
Bartók: *The Wooden Prince*
Tchaikovsky: *Swan Lake*, Second act
Concert programme

Zagreb

1966, November 12, 13
Chopiniana
Concert programme
Bartók: *The Miraculous Mandarin*

Belgrade

1966, November 15, 16
Bartók: *The Wooden Prince*
Concert programme
Bartók: *The Miraculous Mandarin*

Sofia

1966, November 21, 22
Chopiniana
Concert programme
Bartók: *The Miraculous Mandarin*

1966, November 23, 24
Adam: *Giselle*

Vienna

1967, June 8
Bartók: *The Wooden Prince*

Bartók: *The Miraculous Mandarin*

1967, June 9
Bartók: *Music for Strings, Percussion and Celesta*

Wiesbaden

1968, May 1
Bartók: *Dance Suite*
Bartók: *The Miraculous Mandarin*

Helsinki

1968, May 25, 26
Chopiniana
Concert programme
Khachaturian: *Gayane Suite*

1968, May 27, 28
Prokofiev: *Classical Symphony*
Concert programme
Tchaikovsky: *The Sleeping Beauty*, Third act

Bergen

1968, May 30, 31
Chopiniana
Concert programme
Khachaturian: *Gayane Suite*

Berlin

1968, November 27
Bartók: *The Wooden Prince*
Bartók: *The Miraculous Mandarin*

Baalbek

1969, August 29, 30, 31
Khachaturian: *Spartacus*

Paris

1969, November 4, 6, 7, 8
Khachaturian: *Spartacus*

Le Havre

1969, November 10, 11
Chopiniana
Concert programme
Khachaturian: *Gayane Suite*

Bologna

1970, May 2, 4
Chopiniana
Concert programme
Bartók: *The Miraculous Mandarin*

1970, May 6, 7, 9
Adam: *Giselle*

Bucharest

1970, December 16, 19

Chopiniana
Krein: *Laurencia*, Second act
Bartók: *The Miraculous Mandarin* (László Seregi)

1970, December 17, 20
Khachaturian: *Spartacus*

Dortmund

1971, April 29
Bartók: *The Wooden Prince* (László Seregi)
Bartók: *The Miraculous Mandarin* (László Seregi)

DANCES IN THE CONCERT PROGRAMMES PERFORMED
ABROAD SINCE 1961

The Beggar Student
Ballet Interlude
Mus.: Millöcker
Chor.: Seregi

The Flames of Paris
Fourth act, *pas de deux*
Mus.: Asafiev
Chor.: Vainonen

Gayane
Pas de deux
Mus.: Khachaturian
Chor.: Anisimova

The Girl Danced into Life
Film, *pas de deux*
Mus.: Vujicsics
Chor.: Seregi

Giselle
First act, *pas de deux*
Mus.: Adam
Chor.: Lavrovsky

Giselle
Second act, *pas de deux*
Mus.: Adam
Chor.: Lavrovsky

The Hunter and the Bird
Pas de deux
Mus.: Grieg
Chor.: Yakobson

Kerchief
Pas de deux
Mus.: Kenessey
Chor.: Harangozó

Kerchief
Gipsy Scene
Mus.: Kenessey
Chor.: Harangozó

Largo
Mus.: Bach
Chor.: Seregi

Melody
Pas de deux
Mus.: Gluck
Chor.: Messerer

Nutcracker
Third act, *pas de deux*
Mus.: Tchaikovsky
Chor.: Vainonen

Sheherazade
Pas de deux
Mus.: Rimsky-Korsakov
Chor.: Harangozó

The Sleeping Beauty
Blue Bird, *pas de deux*
Mus.: Tchaikovsky
Chor.: Petipa

The Sleeping Beauty
Pas de deux
Mus.: Tchaikovsky
Chor.: Petipa

The Sleeping Beauty
Pas de cinq
Mus.: Tchaikovsky
Chor.: Petipa

Spartacus
Pas de deux
Mus.: Khachaturian
Chor.: Anisimova

Spring
Pas de deux
Mus.: Grieg
Chor.: Barkóczy

Spring Surge
Pas de deux
Mus.: Rakhmaninov
Chor.: Messerer

Swan Lake
Second act, *pas de deux*
Mus.: Tchaikovsky
Chor.: Messerer

Swan Lake
Third Act, *pas de deux*
Mus.: Tchaikovsky
Chor.: Messerer

Taras Bulba
Gopak
Mus.: Soloviev-Sedoi
Chor.: Lopukhov

Valse
Pas de deux
Mus.: Moszkowski
Chor.: Messerer

CONTENTS

PHOTOS BY TAMÁS FÉNER: 6, 12, 14, 15, 24, 25, 26, 28, 29, 30, 32, 33, 34, 35, 36, 38, 41, 54, 68, 70, 77, 89, 91, 92, 95, 96, 97, 99, 101, 102, 103, 105, 106, 107, 108, 109, 110, 111, 112, 113, 114; TAMÁS HORVÁTH (MTI): 10, 21; BÉLA JÁRMAI (MTI): 17, 83, 84, 85, 87; ÉVA KELETI (MTI): 1, 2, 3, 5, 7, 8, 9, 13, 16, 18, 19 20, 22, 27, 31, 44, 45, 46, 47, 48, 49, 50, 52, 53, 55, 56, 57, 58, 59, 63, 64, 65, 66, 67, 69, 71, 72, 73, 74, 75, 76, 78, 79, 80, 81, 82, 86, 88, 90, 93, 94, 104; PÉTER KORNISS: 39, 60, 61; BÉLA MEZEI: 42, 51, 98, 100; ZOLTÁN SEIDNER (MTI): 23; ANDOR TORMAI (MTI): 4, 11; PHOTO MTI: 37, 40, 43, 62

ON THE COVER: *CHOPINIANA*, PHOTO TAMÁS FÉNER
ON THE BACK OF THE COVER: *SPARTACUS*, PHOTO ÉVA KELETI (MTI)

Printed in Hungary 1971
Kossuth Printing House, Budapest
CO667—h—7173

Mattie the Gooseboy
1 Eszti–Adél Orosz, Mattie the gooseboy–
Levente Sipeki
2 Döbrögi–Gyula Harangozó, the Bailiff–
Zoltán Sallai with the wise-women

Mischievous Students
3 Eager-Beaver Joe, the teacher's pet–Levente
Sipeki in the teachers' room
4 The horseherds' dance: from left Imre Eck,
László Kiss and Viktor Róna

Kerchief
5 Gipsy Dance–Zsuzsa Kun and Ferenc Havas

The Wooden Prince
6 The Prince–Viktor Róna, the Princess–
Adél Orosz
7 Viktor Róna and the Wooden Prince–
Sándor Perlusz
8 Adél Orosz and József Forgách
9 Adél Orosz and Viktor Róna
10 The Finale

The Miraculous Mandarin
11 The den of the tramps
12 The Streetwalker–Gabriella Lakatos and the
Old Gallant–Ágoston Balogh
13 Gabriella Lakatos and the Young Student–
József Forgách
14 Gabriella Lakatos and
15 the Miraculous Mandarin–
16 Viktor Fülöp

Polovtsian Dances
17 Group dance

Promenade Concert
18 The Young Girl–Adél Orosz, the Fop–
Zoltán Péter
19 The Maecenas–Gyula Harangozó
20 The Primadonna–Vera Szumrák and the
Maecenas–Ágoston Balogh

Sheherazade
21 Sheherazade–Zsuzsa Kun, the Young Moor–
Viktor Fülöp
22 Sheherazade–Klotild Ugray, the Young
Moor–Levente Sipeki
23 The dance of Odalisques

Coppélia
24 Swanilda–Jacqueline Menyhárt
25 Coppélius–Gyula Harangozó
and Coppélia–Gabriella Lakatos
26 Gyula Harangozó

Chopiniana
27 Grande Valse Brillante
28 Prélude. Zsuzsa Kun
29 Valse. Ildikó Kaszás
30 Mazurka II. Mária Kékesi
31 Grande Valse Brillante

Petrouchka
32 Sándor Perlusz as Petrouchka
33 The three puppets in Scene One–László
Péter, Gabriella Lakatos and Levente Sipeki
34 The struggle of the three puppets–
Ildikó Kaszás, Győző Zilahy and Sándor
Perlusz
35 Levente Sipeki as Petrouchka

Firebird
36 Mária Kékesi as Firebird
37 Mária Kékesi and Ferenc Havas as the
Tsarevitch
38 Zsuzsa Kun as Firebird
39 The Beauty Princess–Erzsébet Gombkötő,
and the Tsarevitch–Imre Dózsa
40 The princesses. Dance with the Golden Apples

Nutcracker
41 Dance of the Snowflakes
42 The Rose Waltz

Swan Lake
43 Act II. Adagio
44 Odette–Zsuzsa Kun, the Prince–Ferenc
Havas
45 Act II. With Maya Plissetskaya and Maris
Liepa, guests from the Bolshoi Theatre
46 Mária Kékesi and Ferenc Havas
47 Zsuzsa Kun

Don Quixote
Pas de deux from Act Three. (Identical
momentum, different personalities)
48 Gabriella Lakatos and Ferenc Havas
49 Zsuzsa Kun and Imre Dózsa

Giselle
50 Giselle–Zsuzsa Kun, Prince Albert–Imre
Dózsa
51 Zsuzsa Kun and Viktor Fülöp as Prince
Albert
52 The dance of the willis
53 Adél Orosz as Giselle and Viktor Róna
as Albert

The Sleeping Beauty
54 Act I. Aurora–Zsuzsa Kun
55 Aurora–Mária Kékesi

LIST OF PLATES